Conversations with Stoppard

Mel Gussow is a critic and author. As longtime drama critic for the New York Times he was a winner of the George Jean Nathan Award for Dramatic Criticism, the only critic ever to win that prestigious award for reviews published in the Times.

He has written Profiles for the New Yorker on Athol Fugard, Bill Irwin, Peggy Ramsay and Michael Gambon. In addition he has done Profiles for the New York Times Magazine about V.S. Naipaul, Dustin Hoffman, Marsha Norman, Alan Ayckbourn and Brian Friel among many others.

Before joining the Times, he was a critic and cultural writer for Newsweek Magazine. The author of *Don't Say Yes Until I Finish Talking: a Biography of Darryl F. Zanuck,* he has taught film at New York University. He was the recipient of a Guggenheim Fellowship and for three years served as the president of the New York Drama Critics Circle. A graduate of Middlebury College, he holds a master's degree in journalism from Columbia University. He has also published a companion volume to this book, *Conversations with Pinter.*

Mel Gussow

Conversations with Stoppard

Grove Press
New York

Originally published in Great Britain by Nick Hern
Books Ltd. in 1995
First Grove Press paperback edition published in July
1996

Published simultaneously in Canada
Printed in the United States of America

Library of Congress Cataloging-in-Publication Data
Stoppard, Tom.
    Conversations with Stoppard / Mel Gussow. — 1st
Grove Press pbk. ed.
        p.   cm.
    Originally published: London: Nick Hern Books,
1995.
    Includes index.
    ISBN 0-8021-3468-8
    1. Stoppard, Tom—Interviews.   2. Dramatists,
English—20th century—Interviews.   3. Playwriting.
I. Gussow, Mel.   II. Title.
    [PR6069.T6Z464   1996]
    822'.914—dc20   96-7190

Grove Press
841 Broadway
New York, NY 10003

10 9 8 7 6 5 4 3 2 1

Contents

For Ann and Ethan

Introduction

In Tom Stoppard's radio play, *Where Are They Now?*, the author's surrogate looks back nostalgically on his schooldays, and defines happiness as 'a passing change of emphasis'. A dozen years later, the protagonist of *The Real Thing* reiterated the statement with his observation, 'Happiness is equilibrium. Shift your weight.' For Stoppard, equilibrium had become a credo, as he repositioned himself to suit the shifts in the world. Call it a Stoppardian sense of gravity. The playwright provides his own ballast, as he tries to remain in the moral centre of his universe. If one needs a symbol of Stoppard's own inner balance, consider the pronunciation of his name. It is STOP-PARD, with the syllables evenly accented.

His life and his work are crowded with apparent contradictions. Although he was born in Zlin, Czechoslovakia (as Tomas Straussler) and spent his early years in Singapore and India, he has become one of the most English of Englishmen. He currently lives both in Chelsea in London and in Iver, Bucks, where he is a country squire, with an English garden, a lawn for cricket, a tennis court and his neighbour's cows peeping through the windows of his house. His idea of Arcadia, of an idyllic environment, is the English countryside. Yet he spends most of his time in cities, is frequently flying from one to another, and has a very cosmopolitan nature. He is one of the wittiest and most literate writers of the English language, but he left school at an early age and found his education while working on a provincial English newspaper. (Coincidentally, none of England's pre-eminent living playwrights, Harold Pinter, Alan Ayckbourn and Stoppard, went to university.) Although he has a gift for inventing epigrams, metaphors and circumlocutions, in his own reading he has great admiration for the understated art of Ernest Hemingway. Stoppard has no background in philosophy, philology, physics, metaphysics, mathematics or circus acrobatics, but his plays are filled with knowledgeable references to these and other specialised fields. In contrast to Pinter and Ayckbourn, he is untutored in the techniques of theatre, except for what he learned during his years as a drama critic and from working with and watching his directors. Yet his plays have a brilliant theatricality. He is, in fact, an exemplary autodidact, and a very quick study.

In the plays, things are never quite what they seem to be. There are plays within plays, and in *The Real Thing*, a play outside the one we are watching. The image is that of an endless series of Chinese boxes or an exercise in recursion. Time plays tricks, as past and present coexist and sometimes brush against each other on the same stage. In many of his plays, there are echoes of his previous writings. The subject matter may shift from moral philosophy to quantum physics, but the voice is that of the author caught in the act of badinage, arguing himself in and out of a quandary. Most of his plays are inspired by a single central image (philosophy as gymnastics, a madman who thinks he has a symphony orchestra in his head). But, as the plays evolve, they become prisms, reflecting and refracting the author's ingenuity. Is Stoppard too clever by half, an intellectual rather than an emotional playwright? He confronts this and related questions during our conversations.

From the moment that Rosencrantz and Guildenstern first appeared in court and wondered what in Elsinore was going on with their eccentric classmate, Stoppard has been questioning man's power of self-determination, his ability to cope within repressive circumstances. This remains one of his principal themes, along with the variability of memory and the unreliability of the lessons of history. *Rosencrantz and Guildenstern Are Dead* marked him as a playwright of ideas, one label that he accepts, but gradually he has revealed a reservoir of emotion beneath the artifice. At the same time, he has demonstrated a greater mastery of character and plot. His plays have become more personal and more resonant, as exemplified by *Arcadia*, in which he consolidates such diverse subjects as horticulture and chaos mathematics into an organic panoply, and by *Indian Ink*, in which he draws upon his own memories of India. He can divide his work between 'madcap comedies' and plays of ideas, but the distinctions are not that clear-cut. He writes madcap comedies of ideas.

One division is simply of length: short quick Stoppard and longer, more contemplative and more complex works. Sometimes the short, like *The Real Inspector Hound*, turns out to be the real thing and enters the international repertoire. Long or short, there is no mistaking a Stoppard play; he defines himself even as he alters his perspective. In terms of subject, he is always unpredictable; one never knows where he will alight next. With his early plays, he found an identity in the world of philosophy, then moved into areas of science. Before he could be categorised, he quickly sidestepped. His latest play, *Indian Ink*, a stage revision of his radio play, *In the Native State*, explores a conflict of cultures and aesthetics.

Along with *Artist Descending a Staircase*, a radio play that was later adapted to the stage, *Indian Ink* is a rare example of a Stoppard media crossover. In most cases, his work is distinct in each dramatic form. His television plays (*Professional Foul*, *Squaring the Circle*) have expressed his concern for human rights. In one of our early conversations, he is dismissive of the concept of theatre as a place for social protest. But it is Stoppard himself who is speaking when the protagonist of *The Real Thing* says, 'I don't think writers are sacred, but words are. They deserve respect. If you get the right ones in the right order, you can nudge the world a little or make a poem which children will speak for you when you are dead.'

However his conservative positions may differ from those of his more liberal peers, they have great respect for his integrity. David Hare says, 'Tom is separated from most of the English playwrights in that, as an immigrant to England, he is unreservedly in love with England and he approvingly quotes Kipling: "In God's lottery, to be an Englishman is to draw first prize." We have a more jaundiced view.' Hare adds, 'I never find him politically narrow. His friendship and encouragement and generosity to writers of all persuasions are legendary. We have more in common than in conflict.'

Not since Shaw has there been a British playwright as concerned with man's mind and morality, although, in contrast to Shaw, Stoppard is not a social reformer. Through his characters, he offers opinions, but he leaves conclusions to his audience. Given enough tightrope, he can argue on both sides of an issue. Coincidentally, both Shaw and Stoppard were critics before they became playwrights. 'I was an awful critic,' says Stoppard. 'I operated on the assumption that there was an absolute scale of values against which art could be measured. I didn't trust my own subjective responses. And I never had the moral character to pan a friend. I'll rephrase that: I had the moral character never to pan a friend.'

Because of his theatrical contributions, Stoppard may be heading towards knighthood, although the idea of Sir Tom conjures an image of an errant knight rushing into battle before he has laced up his boots. For a moment, let us consider the question of Stoppard's boots, in all their metaphysical complexity. In honour of the incompetent journalist William Boot in Evelyn Waugh's *Scoop*, Stoppard adopted the name as a plume during his early days as a reporter. He liked the name so much that he has used it, or some variation, in his plays, often in tandem with his other favourite, Moon. Boots and Moons proliferate in Stoppardland, as in his novel *Lord Malquist and Mr. Moon* and in *The Real Inspector Hound*, in which the drama critics are named Birdboot and Moon. The characters represent two sides of the author's nature, the philosopher and the pragmatist, the intellectual and the entertainer. He used to think of himself as more a Moon, but in his maturity, the polarities have achieved proximity: the difference has become Moot. (Parenthetically, the playwright himself often wears boots. One pair looks rugged, perfect for striding through the bush, but they are pocked with air holes and would be disastrous if worn in a trout stream; during one period of his life fishing was a favourite pastime. Faced with the contradictory nature of his Boot wear, one wants to say, 'Watch your step, Stoppard.')

He wears his influences lightly, like his loose-fitting shirts and jackets, paying homage at the same time he is indulging in travesty. The plays are annotated with allusions to Beckett, Strindberg and Oscar Wilde, at the same time that he practises one-upmanship with Evelyn Waugh. With his gymnastic joy of language, he loves to turn an image on its head and to tantalise an audience with comic conundrums. He is a craftsman as well as an artist. His stage adaptations (of Schnitzler, Molnár and Nestroy) and his film scripts (of Nabokov, Greene and le Carré) merge his sensibility with that of the original author.

His work testifies to the theory proposed by Vaclav Havel that the basis of humour is incongruous juxtaposition. One example would be Stoppard's favourite line of someone else's dialogue (from Christopher Hampton in *The Philanthropist*): 'I have the courage of my lack of conviction,' a telling line in the light of Stoppard's quest for ambiguity. Stoppard was unintentionally describing his own work when he praised Havel for his 'fascination with language, the absurdities saved from mere nonsense by their internal logic, and the playfulness with which it is done – the utter lack of righteousness, petulance or bile.' He offers mockery without malevolence. As Stephen Sondheim says, 'Tom spreads cheer. He does not spread anguish, gloom, bitchery, tension or anxiety.'

That cheer extends from his writing to his conversation, which is fuelled by linguistic adrenalin: words spin. His talk may seem to be on the run. He is impromptu, but he speaks with a literary precision, and a clear knowledge of the value, the differing value, of words. He talks as he writes:

spontaneity shares centre stage with art. Despite his claim of not being a social creature, he has a natural conviviality. He tends to over-commit himself and therefore is wary of making plans too far in advance.

We began talking in 1972, at the time of the New York premiere of *The Real Inspector Hound.* Periodically, we have met since that time, usually in London or New York, and not always for the record. Occasionally others, including John Wood and Mike Nichols, have joined in. The texts of the talks have been edited for clarity and to excise repetition, but otherwise they appear as they occurred. A conversation with Stoppard is, like one of his favourite quotations from *Scoop*, a 'ruminative feast'.

MEL GUSSOW

March 1995

Conversations with Stoppard

April 1972

'Writing dialogue is the only respectable way of contradicting yourself'

In The Real Inspector Hound, *two drama critics, Birdboot and Moon, become inextricably involved in the action while watching a parody of an Agatha Christie mystery. One of the critics is a second-stringer who, among other obsessions, is contemplating killing the first-stringer. During a brief visit to New York for the opening of* The Real Inspector Hound (*on a double bill with* After Magritte), *Stoppard met me for lunch. My first impression was of a long, lanky, modishly attired teacher or graduate student. I began by saying that he had written a play about me.*

TS: Almost everybody thinks it's a play about critics, a play that was written to get even with critics. The fact that those two characters are critics is a very marginal matter to me. It's about two people in an audience getting involved in a play in which they end up dead. Some of the critical parody stuff I wrote before I ever had a play put on. I wrote a rough draft of the play in 1960, but I abandoned it. It was the second thing I wrote.

In a way, it's a play about wish fulfilment, about the danger of getting what you want. I was a second string critic. I started in journalism in Bristol and went around for years actually reviewing the kind of play I'm parodying. I started out to be a glamorous foreign correspondent. Reviewing Agatha Christie plays was merely the first step to lying on my

1

stomach in some Oriental airport while plate glass was smashed by bazookas.

MG: And you never became a foreign correspondent?

TS: I did get to be a first-string critic.

MG: Not by killing your predecessor.

TS: No, I used a different manoeuvre. I was still a second string critic when I wrote my first play. Then I turned freelance. I went to London and joined a magazine for about six or eight months, which was the lifespan of the magazine. My first play was done on television. My financial needs were so small. I wasn't married. I was living in one room. Finally I gave up journalism.

MG: One thing that interested me in the play was the role of the understudy in life.

TS: It's a jokey play. In point of fact, it's almost impossible to write concretely. The trick is to pretend you're writing concretely and ignore everything else. I always insisted *Rosencrantz and Guildenstern* was a play about two people at Elsinore and not about the generalisations you might drag out of it.

MG: Do you think that critics tend to over-read resonances?

TS: That's absolutely true. When somebody is evaluating a play or a painting, what they think they're doing is recognising its references and its relevance and from that drawing a value judgment. What really happens is that you have a kind of instant experiential response to a play – and then you justify it. If you don't like it, you justify that; and if you love it, you justify that.

MG: Did you find yourself doing that when you reviewed plays?

TS: I probably did it, but it was not a self-conscious act. If it were, it would be criminal.

2

MG: That's what the two critics in the play are doing.

TS: But they've decided instantly before the play starts. That's a retrospective judgment on my part. When a playwright is putting lines down on paper, all he's really thinking about is that people shouldn't leave early. That's the absolute priority of plays.

MG: What's the second priority?

TS: That's probably number one and two. Number three is that you've got to march to your own drummer however eccentric you might be. If you read a lot and see a lot, you're bombarded with influences. It's not always easy to write in your own voice. I really think I'm a playwright by historical accident. In the late 1950's, anybody of my age who thought he could break free of the city room started writing plays. It always used to be books; I think it's going to be books again. There was enormous interest in the theatre. The least fashionable playwright was as fashionable as the most fashionable novelist. The guy who wrote *The Straw Dogs* was on the magazine with me. He's written five or six books. He's a very good writer but very few people want to interview him.

MG: That isn't why you write plays.

TS: I suddenly worked this out: I write plays because writing dialogue is the only respectable way of contradicting yourself. I'm the kind of person who embarks on an endless leapfrog down the great moral issues. I put a position, rebut it, refute the rebuttal, and rebut the refutation. Forever. Endlessly. I have strong opinions but an opinion and a policy are not the same thing. We live in an age where the leper is the don't-know. I want to believe in absolute truth: that there's always a ceiling view of a situation.

I was an awful critic because I operated on the assumption there was an absolute scale of values against which art could be measured. I didn't trust my own subjective responses. And I never had the moral character to pan a friend. I'll rephrase

3

that. I had the moral character never to pan a friend. Being short of money, the magazine had this critic Tom Stoppard and a man named William Boot who wrote about the theatre. I was both of them, which embarrassed me because I had this feeling that critics shouldn't meet anybody in the theatre in case the pure platinum of the response would get corrupted. This is about as wrong an attitude as one could have. Critics are not Olympian figures who make distant assessments.

MG: Some are more Olympian than others.

TS: And their assessments are worth less than others. The kind of critic I liked was Tynan, who lived and ate and drank and sat around among actors and writers. If he thought something was terrible, he said it was terrible. He got belted once by an actor on behalf of his girl friend. If I were reviewing books, I couldn't retire into seclusion and not meet people whose books I might review. The kind of scepticism which used to be levelled at the New York Review of Books as the New York Review of Each Other's Books, that's nonsensical.

MG: What's your audience?

TS: I mentally define my audience as people who like the jokes I like. Quite frankly, that doesn't leave out very many people. You don't think of yourself as having some kind of esoteric fixation for a particular kind of gag.

MG: You don't think really of yourself as esoteric or eccentric?

TS: Some of the things I've written have puzzled people a bit but in point of fact they are absolutely traditional straight plays although they are about people who don't know very much about what's going on. *Jumpers* is like that.

MG: What is *Jumpers* about?

TS: The cast includes a number of acrobats and gymnasts who jump around quite a lot, and it also includes a man

4

named Jumper and a moral philosopher who believes in metaphysical absolutes. Jumper is the pragmatist.

MG: Is Jumper an approximation of you?

TS: No. Jumper is the villain. I sympathise much more emotionally with the other character who's named after George Moore, the English ethical philosopher. But the play is exactly what I was talking about, an argument between two points of view, both of which I can see virtue in. Intellectually I can shoot one argument full of holes, so I have this other guy who shoots it full of holes. There's a line in the play, 'Atheism is a crutch for those who can't accept the reality of God.' They found traces of amino acid in volcanic rock – the beginnings of life. Now a straight line of evolution from amino acid in volcanic rock all the way through to Shakespeare's sonnets – that strikes me as possible, but a very long shot. Why back such an outsider? However preposterous the idea of God is, it seems to have an edge in plausibility. And that's really what the play's about.

MG: Can you see two sides to every issue?

TS: To any reasonable issue.

MG: What about Ireland?

TS: That's a good example. Two things seem to me to be indisputable about Ireland. One is that the Catholics have an absolutely genuine grievance and the other is that the IRA are incredibly irresponsible, dangerous maniacs who have to be put on board floating hulks in Belfast Harbour as soon as possible. If I had read all the papers and had gone to Belfast, I still wouldn't know the answer.

MG: Could you say where you stand?

TS: I absolutely firmly believe that what are quite coincidentally known as Christian values are good in themselves and don't need rationalisation. I don't believe that telling the

5

truth and not stealing are mechanistic human conventions which we have evolved by living in groups. They transcend all such notions. Some behaviour is good in itself and some behaviour is bad in itself.

One is continually making choices. It gets to be like binary roulette. You go by gut instinct. I don't respect people who are rigorously consistent. That denotes a kind of atrophy of spirit, a certain complacency. I like people who repudiate everything they've written every five years. Probably up until the age of 50 that's a healthy thing to do.

MG: How do you feel about your own plays?

TS: There's stuff I've written I can't bear to watch. They get rotten like fruit and the softest get rotten first. They're not like ashtrays. You make an ashtray and come back next year and it's the same ashtray. Beckett and Pinter have a lot more chance of writing ashtrays because they've thrown out all the potentially soft stuff. I think Beckett has redefined the minima of what theatre could be.

MG: You mean that in a flattering sense?

TS: Absolutely. In 1956 when *Waiting for Godot* was done in Bristol, Peter O'Toole was in the company. I was immobilized for weeks after I saw it. Historically, people had assumed that in order to have a valid theatrical event you had to have x. Beckett did it with x minus 5. And it was intensely theatrical. He's now doing it with x minus 25. I think Pinter did something equally important and significant. He changed the ground rules. One thing plays had in common: you were supposed to believe what people said up there. If somebody comes on and says 'Tea or coffee?' and the answer is 'Tea,' you are entitled to assume that somebody is offering a choice of two drinks and the second person has stated a preference. With a Pinter play, you can no longer make that assumption. You are forced to consider possible alternatives, such as the man preferred coffee but the other person wished him to have tea, or that he preferred the stuff you make from coffee beans under

6

the impression that it was called tea. There are many different possible interpretations for that scene. All of them had been discounted until Pinter exploited the off centre possibilities.

If anything, I do the opposite. I operate on traditional ground rules. People mean what they say unless the audience is told something in advance, for instance about a poisoned cup of tea. On the whole, I write very traditional plays. I admire traditional values. *The Real Inspector Hound* and *After Magritte* are constructed with a sort of attitude that I imagine Terence Rattigan had toward his plays, that they actually have to work as structures. The absurd and bizarre and incongruous positions in Magritte's art are all placed within an absolutely academic context. He may paint a boulder floating in the sky, but the boulder looks heavy. When he paints an apple in a room, it's an apple you can almost eat. It's that combination that I find utterly admirable in Magritte. The play is in a mild and humble way a homage to him. It's not a literary equivalent. The intention is to exhibit the bizarre set of components, but to do so in a mechanism that is closer to Agatha Christie than to Samuel Beckett.

MG: What is the genesis of *After Magritte*?

TS: I went to see a man who had peacocks. They tend to run away. He was shaving one morning and he looked out the window and saw a peacock leap over the hedge into the road. Expensive animals, peacocks, so he threw down his razor and ran out and caught his peacock and brought it back home. I had been looking for a short piece and I had some vague idea of what I wanted to do. I didn't write about the man or the peacock but about two people who just go by, and, boom, they see this man in pyjamas, with bare feet, shaving foam on his face, carrying a peacock. They see this man for five-eighths of a second – and that's what I write about.

Rosencrantz and Guildenstern is about Hamlet as seen by two people driving past Elsinore. It's a favourite thing of mine: the idea of an absolutely bizarre image which has a total rationale to it being seen by different people. And everybody

7

is absolutely certain about what they see. There are tiny bits of that in *Jumpers*: a man carrying a tortoise in one hand and a bow and arrow in the other, his face covered in shaving foam. A trick I enjoy very much is when, bit by bit, you build up something ludicrous – and then someone walks in.

MG: Have you seen anything bizarre lately?

TS: The first time I was here in New York, on a book of matches it said, '27 things to do with a hamburger.' The same day I was being interviewed by *Look* magazine. The interviewer from *Look* wore an eye-patch . . . I find it terribly difficult to come across something to write about, not in terms of subject matter, in terms of structure. Sometimes idea and structure are indivisible. A friend of mine said, why didn't I write a play about Rosencrantz and Guildenstern? I'm vaguely aware of leaving myself open to that kind of trigger.

MG: What are you working on now?

TS: A radio play. I'm doing another stage play after that. It's on an historical fact of no consequence. I find it so terribly interesting, and I don't know what to do with it. A friend said, 'In 1916 in Zurich living within a stone's throw of each other and using the same café were the Dadaist, Tristan Tzara, and Lenin, and I think Freud, maybe. Look into it.' You have to go through the labour of reading up a bit and writing 18 drafts, and you've got your next play. I think it might be nice to do a two-act thing, with one act a Dadaist play on Communist ideology and the other an ideological functional drama about Dadaists.

Jumpers is, as much as anything, an anti-Skinner play [B.F. Skinner, the American psychologist]. Perhaps I'll call it 'Skinner' in America. Eight Skinners instead of eight Jumpers. Skinner is a highly provocative fascinating intelligent brilliant wrongheaded oaf. If people actually write well and epigramatically and clearly, the ideas gain in authority. That's one of the interesting things about polemical writing. The people who have the reputation as being the best critics are in fact the people with the best prose-style. Skinner says something like, 'The problem is not to make people good but to make them behave well.' That's got an epigrammatic force. How can you refute a statement that's as beautifully put as that? Macaulay has a gigantic reputation as an historian and critic. He could write the socks off his contemporaries, but his history of England was a Whig history. As I said, I've always thought that Tynan was the best critic. He may have been, but not necessarily. He just wrote a lot better.

MG: How do you feel about the reviews for *The Real Inspector Hound* and *After Magritte*?

TS: Everybody likes *The Real Inspector Hound* better than *After Magritte*.

MG: Except you?

TS: I like *Magritte* enormously. It's a very peculiar and fragile thing. I like the way it was done here. I never actually enjoyed a rehearsal as much as this one.

MG: Did you mix in?

TS: I'm a very nosy author. I try to channel things discreetly through the director. With an optimum situation, with the most sensitive director, the best actors and the most brilliant designers, you get about 65 or 70 per cent of what you mean – and that's the top. The other 30 per cent consists of secrets between you and the play. You can't ever get a play on paper like a music score.

MG: Why don't you direct your own plays?

TS: I'm thinking of doing that, if I find something not too difficult to do. I enjoy working with actors enormously, and I'm very dogmatic about how I think things ought to be done. You don't write *à la carte* when you write plays. One writes set menus. Take it or leave it.

April 1974

'Seriousness compromised by my frivolity or . . . frivolity redeemed by my seriousness'

Before Jumpers *opened on Broadway in 1974, we met again, and necessarily the conversation was enlivened by verbal acrobatics and intellectual cartwheels. Stoppard began by talking about our first conversation.*

TS: I thought I'd never do that again. It worked well, didn't it? I'm never pleased with interviews. I do them because it would be churlish to refuse and to make trouble for producers. But that time I actually liked it. I suppose we shouldn't spoil our record by doing another one.

MG: Have you finished your new play?

TS: Yes. It's about Lenin and Joyce and Tzara in Zurich in 1917, but it's not a historical play. We've started rehearsals at the Royal Shakespeare Company. It's overlapping with this, unfortunately. The play is called *Travesties.*

MG: You're going in for plural titles these days.

TS: Yes, with neither the definite nor the indefinite article. It's not a policy, just a habit.

MG: I haven't seen *Jumpers* yet but I read it. Reading it, I feel like an acrobat.

TS: It's not as crazy as it reads. It's got a plot, and, as you noticed, it's got a body of a policeman. It's a whodunit, but you're not told who dun it.

MG: Did you ever decide who did it?

TS: Electricians and stagehands get me into corners and ask. The play's been in Washington eight weeks, and it's driving them mad. They want to know, who did it? It's not about who did it, it's about a fact that's been done. And there are several options. The point of it is really that life doesn't guarantee us a dénouement, and why should you believe the ones you're given in the theatre?

MG: One reason we like dénouement in the theatre is that we don't have it in life.

TS: It would be absolutely perverse to write a conventional whodunit without saying who did it. This particular murder is a strand in a much more general situation, isn't it?

MG: Last time we talked you said you wrote traditional plays.

TS: I think that came out as an affirmative statement. What I really meant: I don't think of myself as the author of absurd plays. Didn't I say something about the kind of plays I don't write? There is a kind of play Terence Rattigan doesn't write – and I don't write it either. That's what I meant. Obviously it would be dumb to deny that they're freer than the purely conventional drawing-room play. On the other hand, they stick by certain narrative rules. It's not a warm bath of images and references. That's the kind I don't write, and I don't go to them either. It's largely a matter of taste. One is always claiming the status of opinion for what is really one's taste. You write what you're best at writing. It would be foolish and doubtless fatal to set out to write a particular kind of play for some quite ulterior motive.

MG: *Jumpers* seems freer than your other plays.

TS: On the page you see a daunting monologue. George opens his mouth at the beginning of the play and he's there for 15 minutes. It looks slightly horrifying, but in fact in Brian Bedford's mouth it's the safest part of the play.

MG: I was speaking less of the monologue than of the whole style of the play, the quick switching from vaudeville and acrobatics to discourse.

TS: Watching it last night, it just works as a comedy. You can't really think of it as a daring advance because 'daring advance' is self-negating. My 'latest daring advance' will play the Billy Rose Theatre!

MG: For a limited engagement of three performances.

TS: At least that would make sense, but you can't say, book now for 'daring advance' now in second year.

MG: But obviously you didn't set out to write 'my latest comedy'. You had deeper, perhaps profound thoughts in mind. What *did* you have in mind?

TS: For once I did have an abstract proposition to write about, which wasn't the case with *Rosencrantz and Guildenstern*, a play about two people in a specific concrete, geographical location. The situation in this play is much better expressed by a proposition such as 'moral values are alternatively purely social conventions or refer to some absolute divinity'. Now that is a proposition which interests me enough to want to write about it. Obviously the very fact that one is writing theatre, as opposed to a thesis, predicates one's attitude to the material. I write for a fairly broad audience, with me plumb in the middle. I don't write for rarefied audiences. I don't think of myself as being rarefied.

I don't write about heroes. I tend to write about oppositions

13

and double acts. I identify emotionally with the more sympathetic character in the play who believes that one's mode of behaviour has to be judged by absolute moral standards. At the same time I don't have to get anyone else to write the other character for me, because intellectually I can shoot my argument full of holes. This conflict between one's intellectual and emotional response to questions of morality produce the tension that makes the play.

A long time ago I had an image of a troupe of gymnasts making a pyramid and there being a gunshot and one gymnast being blown out of the pyramid, the rest of the pyramid imploding on the hole that he left. I had this piece of paper with this dead acrobat on the floor, and I didn't know who he was, who shot him, or why.

MG: Do you know where the image came from?

TS: No. I've never seen it happen. I may have already decided to use the twelve gymnasts in some way, and instead of simply using them to decorate the piece, I wanted to integrate them by making one of them a character in a play, even if the first thing that happens is that he's shot. As you know the gymnasts have two lives; they act two roles in the play. They're the more gymnastic members of the philosophy school and the more philosophical members of the gymnastic team. My objective has always been to perform a marriage between a play of ideas and a farce. As to whether this is a desirable objective, I have no idea. It represents two sides of my own personality, which can be described as seriousness compromised by my frivolity, or . . . frivolity redeemed by my seriousness .

MG: Do you think of philosophy as a balancing act?

TS: To begin with, philosophy doesn't actually impress me as an academic discipline. I think philosophy is actually taking place in a . . . bubble. It wouldn't matter a damn if the bubble were floated out to sea, because it's a self-enclosed world dealing in abstractions. I can appreciate the attraction. I can play chess with myself too. That doesn't mean it's doing anybody any good. On the other hand, most of the propositions I'm interested in have been kidnapped and dressed up by academic philosophy, but they are in fact the kind of proposition that would occur to any intelligent person in his bath. They're not academic questions, simply questions which have been given academic status.

Philosophy can be reduced to a small number of questions which are battled about in most bars most nights. Linguistic philosophy doesn't even have that distinction. It should occupy the position in life similar to that of collecting labels off triangular pieces of cheese. There's a word for people who do that. And they trade cheese labels across continents. It doesn't do anybody any harm, but why would you have a professor of it?

I'm being awfully rude about these people. They're very nice people. I actually met some philosophers after writing the play, and they all impressed me. I'm very proud to know Professor Ayer; his company's a great pleasure. I'm being unnecessarily glib about his chosen academic love. On the other hand, it's much easier to justify someone whose philosophy has to do with society rather than the way we use language. As it happens, it interests me, but to devote one's life to it, to have a chair in it, a faculty in it, a building around it and an examination set in it – it all seems to get out of hand. When I started reading books on moral philosophy, I was just amazed at how many people were writing the same book.

MG: Did you start reading these books once you were writing the play?

TS: I wanted to write a play about this particular conflict between emotional and intellectual responses to the idea of God, because I've always thought that the idea of God is absolutely preposterous but slightly more plausible than the alternative proposition that, given enough time, some green slime could write Shakespeare's sonnets. And then I started reading to make sure that my profound thoughts were not going to be refuted by any first-year philosophy students. It turned out that they *were* the propositions of first-year philosophy students.

I read these books without any kind of feeling of earnest duty. I read them as long as I enjoy them, which was quite a long time. Quite often I found them unconsciously hilarious. There are things in my play which people innocently suppose to be my kind of bizarre version of academic discourse, that I'm doing a Mel Brooks on it, when, in fact, occasionally, I hardly had to change a thing . . . There are certain universal, transcendent virtues which are good in themselves.

MG: Could you name three?

TS: Not really. If you say, being kind is good, the next person asks, what about being kind to Hitler? What this man in the play says is that you can't name it because it isn't another word for being something else, like being kind. The notion of comparing one action to another would be meaningless without the predicate that there is some standard to refer to.

MG: You must have standards yourself.

TS: Well, yes. But that's another matter. Privately there are things that are generally – and rightly – approved of. Being kind is one of them. On the other hand, what Professor Ayer would say is that they're approved of not because of some inherent and divine property but because we have evolved them as a code of conduct to make living in groups a practical possibility. They have their good colour from their usage. He says in the play that it's like the rules of tennis, without which Wimbledon would be a shambles. They evolved because it's the only way to make the game possible.

It's not a play that says there are good people who are theists

16

and bad people who are atheists. Quite clearly, that's nonsense. An atheist can be as good as anybody else. Frequently, better. What the play says is that if the status of goodness is a matter of convenience and social evolution, and consequently, has simply evolved through a series of changes, then it is open to be changed into a reverse direction where casual murder might be deemed good – if somebody had enough power to make it so.

In case you want to write your next book about it: if a dictatorship decreed that it was good conduct to spy on your neighbours and betray them for harbouring subversive thoughts, then even if the entire population subscribed to this conduct as being a virtue, it would still be wrong. In other words, there is a frame of reference, which is quite beyond the total population.

MG: How does that relate to President Nixon?

TS: The great redeeming and reassuring element in this whole Nixon business is that the majority of ordinary people is still capable of recognising an abuse of power not as the norm. If it became the norm and nobody recognised it as an abuse, then you're really in trouble.

It isn't very difficult to demonstrate scientifically that this is the case. You can do it with rats and mice in the laboratory. Given a few cages and a few electrical impulses you can control animal behaviour. The question is whether man is a large animal. Or whether, as this poor professor hopes, there is more in him that meets the microscope. And even the scientist who wields the microscope and sees nothing there, the fact that he's capable of the thought process is suggestive of yet another outside framework. Did I tell you there's a nude lady in *Jumpers* – and singers and dancers? [He laughs.]

MG: What does a nude lady have to do with a play about moral philosophy?

TS: Does it have to?

MG: Is it just to sell tickets?

TS: No, not at all.

MG: But why a striptease on a trapeze?

TS: It's another completely isolated image which I wanted to drag in. I love the idea. It's very theatrical. The only way I really work is to assemble a strange pig's breakfast of visual images and thoughts and try and shake them into some kind of coherent pattern.

MG: Apparently there was a recent pornographic movie in which there was intercourse on a trapeze.

TS: Not easy. [Discouraged.] Already we're old-fashioned.

MG: A striptease on a trapeze is not easy either.

TS: The actress is wonderful. She worked in a circus. She hangs by her teeth, and the great thing is that eight weeks ago she was just someone who swung on a trapeze and took her clothes off. Now her whole performance has blossomed. As a secretary she's doing things with her pencils and her typewriter and her knitting. And I just watch her half the evening. Poor Brian will be delighted to hear that.

MG: As a playwright, you can envision these images and then bring them to life on stage.

TS: Particularly in this production. In England we had eight actors from the National Theatre. Any of them could give you an Horatio, but they were not so good at cartwheels or back flips. Here we have at least 12 guys who can do marvellous things on trampolines. The pyramid is exactly as I imagined it, which it never was in London. First of all, we had four fewer people and secondly you couldn't ask them to do what you could ask them to do here. The pyramid is 18 feet high and really quite frightening. In England, it was 12 feet high.

MG: Perhaps here the critics will say the acrobats are too good.

TS: It's a fair point. Peter Wood quite rightly saw America as the land of opportunity when it comes to gymnastics. Ideally I think they ought to be able to do ineptness brilliantly. Instead of doing ineptness, they're just brilliant. Obviously it's a razor's edge. I personally think there's nothing more wonderful than a brilliant juggler playing a bad juggler.

MG: Can you do acrobatics?

TS: I used to be able to stand on my head. I could never do a cartwheel. I was always an intellectual from the word go.

MG: An intellectual who could stand on his head would be much more in demand than an intellectual who stands on his feet.

TS: I didn't calculate it as such, but this whole thing of gymnastics and standing on one's head and doing somersaults is a fairly good metaphor for philosophical activity. And *Jumpers* is a very good word for bridging between acrobats and conclusions.

MG: Do you feel there's no function to philosophy? Is it just an exercise?

TS: I think that Wittgenstein said that philosophy wasn't a subject, it was an activity. Nowadays it's largely an analytical activity. I think I have to tread carefully here because I don't really believe mental activity can be dismissed as being useless. But it's not that easy to define what its use is. It's essentially retrospective; it doesn't really prognosticate; it doesn't really shape and define what's coming up. All I can say is that survival is going to depend on good brains, so one shouldn't knock the activity. It's perfectly natural that the search for meaning should exist.

19

MG: People who don't like your work would say that you indulge in intellectual exercises.

TS: I don't subscribe to the proposition that the plays are activities in themselves. My plays are so near the knuckle of life. [Laugh.] If you looked out of your window and saw something that you really felt must be changed, something you felt was a cancer on society and you wanted to change it *now*, you could hardly do worse than write a play about it.

MG: What would you do if you wanted to change something?

TS: What Woodward and Bernstein did. I hope to God they can't do what I do, or otherwise I'm really in trouble. There's a reporter in England who just won an award for a series he did on South Africa for the Guardian. He wrote a story on wages paid by British companies in South Africa. The Guardian ran this piece months ago. Now within 48 hours the wages have gone up. I can't do that. I'll never be able to do that. Athol Fugard will never be able to do that, not by writing plays. What the hell am I doing then? The answer is very simple, and I think it's very important. I think that art provides the moral matrix *from* which we draw our values about what the world ought to be like. In other words, it's because of people like Athol Fugard that the editor of the Guardian realised that the reporter's piece was worth leading the paper with. To stretch a point: our moral sensibility is laid down by art not by reportage. Fugard is part of a long-term activity which lays down people's sense of good and bad. Not all art does that.

MS: Aren't there artists who can, through their lives, do something in these areas, people like Solzhenitsyn?

TS: Absolutely. It's worth asking whether the artist and the revolutionary can be the same person or whether the activities are mutually exclusive.

MG: Do you mean political revolutionary?

TS: Yes. Somebody who can change the world. How would you justify *Ulysses* to Lenin? Or Lenin to Joyce?

MG: Can the artist be a revolutionary?

TS: There have been artists who were revolutionary. Like Mayakovsky, who was celebrated in Russia before the Revolution as an avant-garde poet. He became the laureate of the Revolution. Even in translation, it comes over as superior propaganda poetry. There were two of him fighting for the pen . . . Your art is defined by what you are, to a very large extent. I'm an English middle-class bourgeois who prefers to read a book to almost anything else. It would be an insane pretension for me to write 'poems of a petrol bomber'.

MG: Have there been any plays that have changed the course of history?

TS: There are two ways of looking at it. Either you can say they did it – or the time was right for the play. It is said that Alexander II freed the serfs in 1861 partly after reading Turgenev's *Sportsman Sketches*, short pieces about Russian peasantry. Probably what happened was that the time was right for the book and for the freeing of the serfs. Didn't Galsworthy's *Justice* have some effect on the law? What about Upton Sinclair? *The Jungle*, if you like, is journalism between hard covers.

MG: Would you like to write a play that would change the course of the world and of art?

TS: I can't even imagine a play doing that.

MG: *Waiting for Godot* has had a lasting effect on theatre.

TS: Absolutely. I don't mean this literally, but I have this feeling that I could have written most other people's plays and most other people could have written mine, because I know how it's done and they know how it's done. But with one or two people – I think Harold Pinter is an example – you don't know how it's done. And I couldn't do it.

MG: Do you feel you've redefined anything in theatre?

TS: Even to ask that question is a curious form of flattery, because it implies one has a sort of historical perspective. It's what I do. I think of myself as having parallel professional lives. Now I only write plays I want to write. But I've written 75 episodes of a serial translated into Arabic, which has no further or prior existence in the English language. I think a writer should think of himself, apart from anything else, as a professional craftsman. You call in a plumber – or a writer.

MG: Was that serial ever done in England?

TS: No. It was about ten years ago and it was a marvellous pay-the-rent job. It really saved my life. I used to have to do five episodes every two weeks. I did it on a Friday to Monday morning, just sat there typing. It was a BBC overseas thing. Another writer and I took turns doing five episodes. No point looking for the nuance. By the time you get into Arabic, where is it?

MG: Will you write another novel?

TS: It's much less pain and trauma than the theatre. There are crises and ambushes waiting for me in theatre.

MG: David Storey spends years on a novel, but writes plays quickly, sometimes in two weeks.

TS: I've never written a play in two weeks. Once I wrote a television play in five days. I wrote *Jumpers* over a period of two years. *Travesties* took last year. I began in March and finished in January.

MG: Did you do lots of research about Lenin and Joyce?

TS: I did do a great deal. But I've taken the precaution of setting the play within the memory of an old gentleman who cannot be totally relied upon for accuracy.

MG: You said you might direct your next play.

TS: A year ago I directed *Born Yesterday* off West End with Lynn Redgrave. I didn't know enough about the play, not having written it. It would be much easier, albeit with pitfalls, to direct a play I'd written. You know the author. You sleep with the author's wife. On the other hand, if I had directed *Jumpers*, it could well have been a disaster. There is a kind of author's blindness.

MG: But you have a picture of what the play is like.

TS: My picture has very few concessions in it. When I wrote *Rosencrantz and Guildenstern*, it could have taken place in a whitewashed basement. When it was taken away and then given back to me, it had collected to itself this vast cobwebbed Gothic chamber and corridors and specially composed music and the best lighting man in the country. One boggles at the whole thing. It was probably essential to it at the time. I think now it would be easier to do it very plain, because the play has an edge to start with. I don't really consider problems of directing when I'm writing a play. I write little stage directions which are like little time bombs that go off in the director's hands when he picks them up. In *Jumpers*, there is a scene change and it just says, 'The bedroom forms around her.' Those five words occupied fine brains for five weeks until the bedroom formed around her. It sort of walks in on her.

I'm looking forward to *Travesties* because it has eight people and they speak. It's going to be a relief after the physical complexity of *Jumpers*.

MG: What's the next play after *Travesties*?

TS: Oh, God. I haven't even the feeling I have a next after *Travesties*.

MG: No unused images?

TS: I wrote a 25-minute opening ceremony for a little lunchtime theatre for a friend of mine. It consisted of some people building a wall and using a private language which grew out of something in Wittgenstein's philosophical investigations. It was five years between *Rosencrantz* and *Jumpers*. Too long. It's only been two years between *Jumpers* and *Travesties*.

MG: Don't your one-acts count?

TS: They do count. They don't count the same way. It's not that the plays are short, it's that they're fundamentally jokes. They're musical boxes, mechanical contrivances. They're not plays about characters.

MG: Why is *Travesties* at the RSC?

TS: Beneath this carefully cultivated modest exterior I'm ravenous for vain publicity. I want to have *Travesties* on at the Royal Shakespeare when they revive *Jumpers* at the National Theatre, and I hope to have a play in the West End and a radio play at the same time. One night I'm going to wipe everybody out.

October 1975

'What is your greatest superstition?' 'It's bad luck to talk about it'

A s a curtain raiser to Travesties, *Stoppard and the play's star John Wood met in an anteroom at the Ethel Barrymore Theatre and batted a dialogue back and forth. I barely edged in a question. Alter egos, kindred spirits with tall spindly bodies, they have known each other for years.*

TS: What sort of interview should this be? The fly on the wall? One with wit and irony?

JW: I never make a joke. Once a year I make a joke. My joke for this year...

TS: Are you superstitious?

JW: Very.

TS: What is your greatest superstition?

JW: It's bad luck to talk about it.

MG: When and where did you first meet?

JW: On the BBC.

TS: I wrote a television play [*Teeth*] about a dentist who finds sitting in his chair a man who has slept with his wife. Half an hour later the man walks out of the office with green teeth and gaps.

JW: As a result of that role I became one of the six most promising dentists in all of England.

TS: And I started writing plays entirely about dentists.

JW: Everybody has one good dentist play in him.

TS: . . . to be extracted.

JW: Actually I was in the early television version of *Jumpers*.

TS: Protojumpers.

JW: It was a live transmission. I had a temperature of 104 and I dried on the first line. I thought it was the end of my relationship with Tom Stoppard. In fact it was the beginning of . . . many dries to come.

TS: I wrote *Travesties* for John. It's hard not to write a play for him. I write plays for somebody who can speak long speeches quickly.

JW: Without appearing to do so.

TS: Miriam [Stoppard's wife] thinks that the fact we're both Cancer is significant. That suggests compatibility. It's not compatibility, but a projection of self. I can't act, so I had to find someone who was tall, thin, neurotic and voluble to act for me.

JW: Contrary-wise, I'm a born playwright.

TS: John was famous when he was about 20 years old. His *Richard III* blew Harold Hobson's mind. He's a sort of genius, and there you are.

JW [embarrassed]: I'm really sort of dishevelled inside and out.

TS: He's too intelligent to rest on being a genius. He finds the optimum possible in my writing. If he finds something not worthy of my eternally questing spirit, he changes it.

JW: I feel like some idiotic Nana. The dog. Not Zola.

TS: Not the dog, the Zola.

JW: Possibly the greatest sacrifice Tom made for me was to shelve *Travesties* while I did *Sherlock Holmes*. It was a hot property in 1974. It's an even hotter property now.

MG: How does it feel to have something written for you?

JW: I recognise *nothing* that can be called writing for me. I operate on blind faith and knowing my friend is a genius. He knows what I'm doing. So away we go. [Exits.]

TS: Originally it was a play about Lenin and Tristan Tzara. I knew what Lenin looked like, so John had to be Tzara. Then I discovered that Tzara was a small dapper man so I had to find another way. Then I discovered that James Joyce was also in Zurich. John was Joyce for a while. I hadn't written a word. Then I was reading Ellmann's biography of Joyce and I came across this Carr figure [a minor official in the British consulate in Zurich]. He's tall! So I wrote a play about Carr. Gods being gods, I said, if he was tall, John could play him. As it turned out, Mrs. Carr is still alive, and she sent me a photo of her late husband, whom I thought I invented. He did actually look like John. Joyce, Tzara and Lenin were all in Zurich at the same time. It's not true they met or were aware of each other's existence. Naturally I had to percolate the whole thing through this man's fallible memory. The thing about Carr playing Algernon [in *The Importance of Being Earnest*] was historical fact.

29

After *Rosencrantz and Guildenstern*, I was asked if I were going to write another play about another play. A play about the fourth spear-carrier in *Oedipus Rex*? When you think of the incredible luck to discover that Joyce put on *The Importance of Being Earnest*. The figure of Joyce seems to correspond to Lady Bracknell who is Lady Augusta. Joyce's middle name was Augustus and through a clerical error he was registered at birth under the name James Augusta Joyce. In the play Tristan Tzara is in the role of Jack Worthing. In Joyce's production, the author who played Worthing was Tristan Rawson. It's a play about a man who wishes to keep control of the other characters.

JW [returning]: I discovered that Algie was a completely funny part at the age of five. I didn't discover I could make people laugh until I was 21 or 22.

TS: That was in *Richard III*. I've never been a performer. I did a radio panel show and got a laugh. Rose petals fell from the sky!

JW: I've been trying to get Tom to take a curtain call.

TS: I once took a curtain call in Hamburg after *Enter a Free Man*. I was roundly booed from the gallery.

JW: There's a story, perhaps apocryphal: in the 1890's there was a touring company of *Hamlet* in the provinces and after a performance the audience said, author author. They pushed a stagehand onstage and someone shot him.

TS [becoming contemplative]: I get emotionally involved in *Travesties*. It disposes of a few private debates of mine. It doesn't have a great sort of parabola, it impinges on a number of topics that preoccupy me from time to time. I think I enlist comedy to serious purpose. I wonder if I don't trivialise something serious. I think there will come a time when I will not want to write in comic terms.

JW: I regret the semantic division between comedy and whatever. I tend to be more mystical. Anything you do is comedy. *Lear* is comedy. The only possible reaction to the human condition is laughter.

TS: I don't agree. That's a Dadaist statement, Theatre of the Absurd time.

July 1979

'The dissident is a discordant note in a highly orchestrated society'

*I*n *the summer of 1979, Stoppard's work was all over London. It was the culmination of 18 months of nonstop activity, which also included the writing of the screenplay for the film version of Graham Greene's* The Human Factor. Night and Day *was a hit on the West End, his adaptation of Schnitzler's* Undiscovered Country *was in repertory at the National Theatre, his political cartoon* Dirty Linen *was in the middle of a long run and a pair of short comedies,* Dogg's Hamlet, Cahoot's Macbeth, *inaugurated the new British American Company. In late July* Every Good Boy Deserves Favour, *a 'play for actors and orchestra,' with music by André Previn, would open at the Metropolitan Opera House in New York. Several weeks before that opening, we talked in London. Because* Every Good Boy *dealt with the subject of dissidence and censorship, I asked him if people were taking him and his work more seriously.*

TS: I'm not taking myself more seriously. For circumstantial reasons it may give that impression. I wasn't sitting there saying I want to write a piece about a Russian dissident. André Previn said, would you like to write a piece for an orchestra? I had to write a piece for a small number of actors and a large orchestra. At first I decided it would be about a zillionaire who had his own orchestra; after supper, the musicians would troop in to play. Then I thought, he could be a zillionaire who thinks he has an orchestra. Once the

33

orchestra was there he didn't have to be a zillionaire, he could be a lunatic. Coincidentally I read about people locked away in insane asylums for political reasons. Suddenly two things came together. The subject matter seemed appropriate to the form: the dissident is a discordant note in a highly orchestrated society.

MG: *Professional Foul* [his television drama about suppression and censorship behind the Iron Curtain] was a different story.

TS: I wanted to write a play for Prisoner of Conscience Year. After a lot of false starts, I wrote this play about a professor who goes to Prague. He's not somebody who's committed to acts for the cause of human rights.

MG: It might be said that you and Woody Allen are having parallel careers, as humorists ripening into serious artists.

TS: I've had the opposite experience. The boot is on the other foot. All along I thought of myself as writing entertainments, like *The Real Inspector Hound* and plays of ideas like *Jumpers*. Confusion arises because I treat plays of ideas in just about the same knockabout way as I treat the entertainments. I can't say that about *Night and Day*. That was a play promised to Michael Codron, and he puts plays on the West End. A play with fifteen acrobats would be of no value to him. I wanted to write a storytelling play. To do *Travesties* again would be a bore. I've always wanted to write a play about journalism. I don't have a lot of ideas. I've been a journalist. It's absurd not to write about journalism sooner or later. My primary problem is not what the play should be about on an abstract level, but who are the people in it – their gender, their age – and where are they? Are they in Africa or in the reporter's room in Bristol? I was interested in people endangering their lives in what is ostensibly a commercial enterprise. The whole thing, why free journalism is important, became a minor obsession.

I don't write plays with heroes who express my point of view. I write argument plays. I tend to write for two people rather than for One Voice. Rosencrantz and Guildenstern were two sides of one temperament. When I start writing, I find it difficult, except on simple questions, to know where I stand – even in *Travesties* in the argument on art between James Joyce and Tristan Tzara. Temperamentally and intellectually, I'm very much on Joyce's side, but I found it persuasive to write Tzara's speech. Faced with the problem of writing a scene, I found things to say for Tzara. In *Jumpers*, George Moore represents a morality that I embrace, rather than that of Archibald Jumper, but both protagonists spoke for me. This is also true of *Night and Day*. There are various things said by various people that I agree with. The things I write are not consistent enough to keep an interview tidy.

MG: What kind of playwright are you?

TS: In general terms, I'm not a playwright who is interested in character with a capital K and psychology with a capital S. I'm a playwright interested in ideas and forced to invent characters to express those ideas. All my people speak the same way, with the same cadences and sentence structures. They speak as I do. When I write an African president into a play, I have to contrive to have him the only African president who speaks like me.

MG: What if you were writing an American play?

TS: All the Americans would have to be educated at Sandhurst or Christchurch – Rhodes scholars discussing John Wayne.

MG: Doesn't that limit you?

TS: It limits me in areas I'm not interested in expanding.

MG: What was your interest in adapting Schnitzler?

TS: What it wasn't was a long interest in Austria and Austrian drama in general and Schnitzler in particular. What it was – while rehearsing *Night and Day* in a church hall in Chelsea, I saw a copy of a literal translation of *Undiscovered Country* on Peter Wood's table. I was just being nosy. They had asked somebody to adapt it, but he pulled out. My interest was partly because Peter Wood would direct it and John Wood would act in it. Once I read the play, I agreed with Peter. It was remarkable, a play completely unknown in England and worthy to stand with Ibsen and English contemporaries. I might have found myself doing whatever was on Peter Wood's table – Molnar, Feydeau, little-known Ibsen.

A woman in San Francisco did my translation of *The House of Bernarda Alba* and assumed I had a great feeling for Lorca and that play in particular. Robin Phillips had just said, could you do two or three weeks' work? With *Undiscovered Country* I started by doing an obsessively faithful first draft – accurate but actable.   Considerably shorter. It is a bit titivated. For someone like me, who enjoys writing dialogue but has a terrible time writing plays, adaptation is joy time. It's a craftsman's job, not 'my soul speaks through Schnitzler.' You go around with a bag of tools doing jobs between personal plays. I really enjoy doing film scripts because you can have someone like Graham Greene invent the story and character, parts I don't enjoy.

MG: What is the relationship between *Dogg's Hamlet* and *Cahoot's Macbeth*?

TS: The first play can be done without the second but the second cannot be done unless it's seen with the first one first. Events and characters from the first play invade the second play. You're even more baffled if you haven't seen the first play. The second play was being written while the first play was being rehearsed. I always wanted to write a play about Ernest Hemingway. I was very taken with his writing when I was a late teenager. I know a great deal about him. So . . .

elegant economy strikes again! Then I realised, I knew a great deal, but I had nothing to say about him.

I was still looking for a play to go with the first half. The good fortune of one's rolling life: in Prague, Pavel Kohout told me about a living-room *Macbeth*. Why don't I write a play about someone trying to do *Macbeth* and getting interrupted? *Dogg's Hamlet* was written for a bus. Ed Berman had the idea of taking plays on a London bus, throwing out the first two seats. I thought about adapting *War and Peace*. In the end, I did *Hamlet*. A 15-minute *Hamlet*. I'm waiting for the right moment to do a five-minute *War and Peace*.

MG: You've been criticised by the left wing as being right-wing. Where do you stand politically?

TS: I try to be consistent about moral behaviour. Let other people hang labels. It's a tactical distortion to label certain attitudes right or left. I'm a conservative with a small c. I'm a conservative in politics, literature, education and theatre. My main objection is to ideology and dogma – Holy Writ for adherents. My plays don't break rules. If you take the orchestra away from *Every Good Boy*, it is a series of scenes telling a coherent story. I don't write Terence Rattigan plays but I think I have more in common with Rattigan than with Robert Wilson. We attempt to be coherent tellers of tales. In *Travesties*, a lot of odd things happen, but the crucial thing is that the whole play is filtered through the memory of an old man – and the audience knows it. I don't want to write utterly conventional plays. Plays are events rather than texts. They're written to happen, not to be read.

July-December 1983

'Happiness is equilibrium. Shift your weight'

*I*n the fall of 1982, The Real Thing *opened in the West End,
in a production starring Roger Rees and Felicity Kendal.
The play was definably Stoppardian in its shifting patterns of
truth and illusion, past and present, while also dealing more
directly with matters of love, marriage and betrayal. It was in
fact his first romantic comedy and an answer to those critics
who thought his previous plays were several steps removed
from life as we know it. The play begins with a scene of
marital discord, as brittle as anything written by Noël
Coward. It is, as we soon learn, fictional, not* The Real
Thing, *but a scene in a play written by a playwright whom we
meet in the second scene. The opening sets the tone for an
evening in which life imitates and contradicts art. The
characters are bonded in conjugality, infidelity and theatre.
Because the protagonist is a playwright, a great deal of the
commentary deals with the use and the abuse of words.*

*One warm afternoon in July 1983, Stoppard and I met for tea
at Brown's Hotel in London, sharing a banquette that
resembled a palanquin. Because of the heat, he removed his
jacket and stuffed it under him, dealing a final death blow to
his sartorial image. Despite the fact that he may wear
fashionable clothes, he often looks as if he is about to ride an
elephant at the head of a column of Gurkhas. His wife
Miriam, a physician and best-selling author of self-help
books, was in another part of the hotel being interviewed in
conjunction with her forthcoming book on being over 50
(neither she nor her husband had reached that age). That*

evening they were due to go to the opera at Covent Garden. Late in our talk, she stopped by to say hello.

We began talking about The Real Thing.

MG: In one of our previous conversations, you said that your plays start with an image, usually visual. Was that true with *The Real Thing*?

TS: I wanted to write a play in which the first scene was written by a character in the second scene.

MG: Was it always going to be a play about a playwright?

TS: No, on the contrary, I put off writing it because I didn't want to write a play about a playwright. That seemed to be the end of the rope: you write a play about someone who's trying to write a play. The genesis of the play was a thing I came across in W. H. Auden's chapbook. In the play, Henry [the playwright] says that public postures have the configuration of private derangement. That's a version of a sentence I read in this Auden chapbook. The idea is that you have a man on stage going through a situation. It turns out he's written it. Then you have the actor in the scene going through the same situation, except he reacts differently. Then you have the guy who wrote it going through the exact situation and he reacts differently too. It's quite a schematic idea. When I was writing the stage directions, I took pains to make sure the geography of doors and furniture remained consistent so that you didn't miss the point. That turned out to be quite unnecessary, you didn't have to worry too much about it.

MG: Reading the text it is quite difficult to visualise it on stage.

TS: I didn't visualise it either. I don't think I would have been brave enough to say I want seven panels to come down in a row. Peter [Wood] wanted a seamless production. He felt the panels were a way of bridging from scene to scene without the show stopping. . . .Writing a play about a playwright is like a painter drawing a picture of someone painting.

MG: People will think it's autobiographical.

TS: I don't know if it's autobiographical, but a lot of it is auto something. Henry sounds off on the subject of writing in exactly the same way the reporters in *Night and Day* said what I wanted to say about journalism.

MG: They're your spokesmen?

TS: It's not their function in either play. The play doesn't exist in order to make those points. I think *Night and Day* is different. There were certain things I wanted to say about journalism. This play wasn't written in order to say certain things about writing. It was written because I liked the idea of the game, the device of having the same thing happen two or three times.

MG: But it does deal more directly with theatre than your other plays.

TS: Yes. But once you're stuck with him being a playwright who wrote the first scene, whatever narrative you invent would be about his life.

MG: He doesn't have to be married to two actresses.

TS: He does, you see.

MG: Not all playwrights are.

TS: I'm not talking about that. I'm talking about my scheme, my idiotic game, a play where it turns out a woman is married to the man who wrote the first scene. If the writer's wife has got to be in both situations, she's got to be an

41

actress. It's determined by the playful idea of having people repeat their situation in fiction. For instance, the Felicity Kendal part, there's a love scene with a person who becomes her lover except in fact they're in *'Tis Pity She's a Whore*. As soon as you decide that's what's going to happen, the woman in the rail scene has got to be an actress because she ends up acting in *'Tis Pity She's a Whore*. That's where the horse is, and that's where the cart is.

MG: Reality imitates art as well as art imitating reality?

TS: I really didn't want to write about actresses or writers, given the choice. Very recently, I was asked to write a Backstage Drama for three different actresses, about being actresses. It's an idea which has no appeal to me of any kind.

MG: *The Real Thing* doesn't deal very much with actresses, but it does deal with the creative process and with theatre as it does or does not imitate life.

TS: I can't remember how much of the play was pre-planned, how much of it was built into the original idea, or whether it just developed that way. I remember, before I began writing anything, I thought the play would be a joke about set design. You could have a scene taking place that is recognisable to the audience as being a real place, and that would turn out to be fake. Then you could have a scene, sort of abstract black, which would be in the conventional theatre. But the whole thing got too complicated. One of the things we had to do when we started previewing was put more information in at the beginning of Scene Two because they found the first scene completely acceptable. Some people didn't catch on.

MG: And they wondered where they were in the second scene?

TS: Exactly. They assume that's the man she ran off with; you're supposed to think that. And the other man came back. By the time the audience caught on, they rather resented it.

Strange really, because there are very naked lines near the beginning of the scene, which give it away even more than we want to. There's a line there that makes me wince every time I hear it. He spells it out for children, talking about 'my wife playing with your husband six times a week and twice on Saturdays'.

MG: Do you need it?

TS: We found in previews that we really did need it, which was so disappointing.

MG: Do you know what Mike Nichols will do differently in the Broadway production?

TS: I have no idea at all. The principle is that New York is a foreign country, and I think foreigners should do the play.

MG: I was wondering about your American audience. You have a strong following outside of New York and also Off Broadway – but on Broadway except for *Rosencrantz and Guildenstern* you haven't had a major success.

TS: That's true. Is it in one's control?

MG: How important was Noël Coward to you in your writing of the play? I was thinking of the first scene and the Norfolk remark.

TS: The first scene was not intended to be a pastiche. I can see there's a resemblance to Coward, but it's not that close. The idiom of acting makes it seem a bit Cowardish.

MG: How do you feel about your fellow playwrights?

TS: Last week this very big book came from America, *British Playwrights 1940 to 1980*, or whatever it was, one of a series of encyclopedias. My agent is also Charles Wood's agent, and he was looking through it and it says, 'Charles Wood,

1931 to 1978. The death of Charles Wood has robbed the British theatre of one of its most interesting voices.' It went on for about 5000 words in the past tense. And there's Charlie living in Oxford.

The last play that I saw by a contemporary playwright, not counting *Steaming*, was *Map of the World*. I think Hare is such a good writer. He writes superb dialogue. I had a card from him. His play and my play have certain structural problems.

MG: You call each other in for rewrites?

TS: I haven't asked him to do mine, and I don't know what to do about his.

MG: Pinter's a friend.

TS: Yes. I'm playing cricket the end of the month for Harold's team . . . I also fish. Michael Hordern and I share fishing on a river in Berkshire. It's a club with a certain number of rods. Michael and I constitute one rod, a weekday rod, so we can fish Monday to Thursday.

MG: Don't you want to be a full rod?

TS: No, once a week is just fine with me; it's as much fishing as I need.

MG: Do you fish in a boat?

TS: No, it's just in a river.

MG: You wade out with high boots?

TS: Yes, yes.

MG: Do you cook it and eat it?

TS: My son is a very keen angler and a keen cook, so he or Miriam does the cooking. I've never cooked a fish. You don't always catch anything. It's nice, though: you walk miles while you're fishing. It's good exercise, and it happens in very agreeable surroundings usually. I work every day, more or less. If I owe something to somebody, I start in the middle of the morning and keep going until the middle of the afternoon and work in the evening. If I don't owe anybody anything then I don't bother working in the evening. It's Parkinson's Law, isn't it? If you've got a lot of work to do, you get rid of your correspondence in 20 minutes; if you've got no work to do, correspondence takes two and a half hours.

MG: Do you watch Wimbledon?

TS: I love sport on television.

MG: Have you ever heard Wimbledon on radio? It's bizarre.

TS: How strange you should say that. I thought exactly the same thing. It's absurd. The man's talking like crazy and he tells you everything and it means nothing. What's the answer to radio tennis? Maybe they should just play music and every 15 seconds say '15 love.'

[Miriam Stoppard, finished with her interview, stops by.]

MS: I don't think anybody's actually written about the hazards of multiple interviews. Your brain flags. You think: brain, send the message! They asked, 'How did you spend your Sunday?'

TS: Planting.

MS: They asked me what I eat for lunch.

TS: What did you say, 'A Big Mac?'

45

MS: I wouldn't *dare*. The interview was for Health and Fitness magazine.

TS: I had my haircut. Did you notice?

MS: I was looking at your hair and I thought it needed cutting.

TS: I was early. I walked around the corner and thought, what am I going to do now? I went into this place called Truefit and Hill and said to tidy it up a little bit.

MS: They took you at your word.

TS: I can mend it . . . I'll tell you what my problem is: a laid-back modesty in my middle age. I'm very garrulous when talking about somebody else, but when I'm interviewed about myself, a curtain falls.

MS: That's what I mean by brain flag.

TS: There's a wonderful remark that Max Beerbohm made about Frank Harris, who was a very famous liar. Somebody wondered if Harris ever told the truth and Beerbohm said, 'Occasionally. When his invention flags.' Like interviews, really.

S toppard lives 40 minutes from London in a small town not too far from Heathrow Airport, from which he makes quick hops to other countries to catch up with productions of his plays and his various television and film projects. His house, at the end of a gravelled drive, hidden from the road by tall trees, has a stately appearance. He lives there with his wife and his four sons.

As invited, I arrived at noon. A housekeeper appeared and led me to the living room. It is a large, airy, pastel-coloured room with many bookcases, the kind of setting in which Alistair Cooke would be comfortable while introducing Americans to still another 'Masterpiece Theatre'. Stoppard is a bibliophile. One bookcase is filled with garden and fitness books, including those written by his wife; another, behind glass, with very fine old editions of Dickens and others. On one shelf are thin leather-bound volumes of his own plays: Rosencrantz and Guildenstern Are Dead, Travesties, Jumpers, Night and Day. The Real Thing *had not yet reached its eternal reward in leather.*

Where Rosencrantz *takes off from* Hamlet, *and* Travesties *bowed to* The Importance of Being Earnest, The Real Thing *stands alone, or as Stoppard summarises it with a certain pride: 'No coat-tails.' The play is also his most personal work. Because of his choice of a playwright as protagonist, it is irrevocably bound up with the life of the author.*

While I was contemplating that fact, the Real Thing walked in the door – tall, shaggy, ebullient and bearing apologies. He was late because he had picked up his son Barnaby at school. He offered me a beer, and then disappeared. The playwright seemed on the verge of becoming elusive. Sometime later, he returned and we strolled to his studio in a converted stable.

*On the first floor, two secretaries (his and hers) were busily
at work. Atop a red, firehouse-style circular staircase was a
long library-like room as burnished as a mahogany barge.
Prominent in the room were a music stand, cricket bat and an
Eames chair cushioned with a crocheted pillow reading*
Jumpers. *On a wall were framed letters of Thackeray,
Tennyson, Strachey and Kipling, along with one of his most
treasured possessions, a personally inscribed photograph of
Samuel Beckett. Two desks faced each other. Any writer
would sell his agent for a study like this.*

MG: Do you write on a computer?

TS: No, with a fountain pen. I was offered a word processor
by Olivetti in return for doing an advertisement. I said no. I
don't want a word processor. It's not the way I work. I write
my plays with my own pen, but in the end there had to be
something legible. Typing them out was a terrible chore. It
finally became so arduous that I managed to swallow my
embarrassment about actually talking my stuff. I dictate onto
a tape. I read what I've written – pages and pages of ink –
and Jacky types from the tape, and then I correct.

MG: So there's an original cast recording of every play.

TS: With me playing every part. A man in the book business
heard about it and said, 'Do you keep the tapes?' I just wipe
them immediately and tape over them. I have about a dozen
cassettes lying about which I use in random order. Very often
I pick up a cassette to dictate a letter and I find my voice
coming back at me with the lines of a play three years old.

MG: A kind of aural palimpsest: painting over painting.

TS: That's right. The painting's still there because we've got
it in the files.

MG: Do you find that you change the play as you read it to
the tape recorder or do you do it word for word?

TS: I find it too time consuming to write down all the stage directions exactly as they ought to be. It's not writing, it's just labour. A lot of them I have in my mind, pictures which I can describe without having to write anything down in the first place. What I write is the dialogue and a few squiggles and shorthand, which I don't need myself because I know what's happening. When I tape the dialogue, I'm continually inserting improvised stage directions. Once it's typed it's harder to change things psychologically. I probably miss a little bit. If I did my own typing, I might change things as I typed. But as Jacky types my tape, that doesn't happen. And once she's typed it, it might as well be carved into marble. There it is: typed. Do I really have a good reason for changing this? It all comes out the same because in rehearsal one becomes completely ruthless about changing it.

MG: How does a radio play differ from a stage play?

TS: Ideally a play in a particular medium should only work in that medium. It should be impossible or pointless to make a movie of a stage play or to make a stage play out of a radio play. In fact, these lines are often crossed. Several days ago, someone asked if they could do a stage play of one of my television plays. Some of my radio plays have been done on stage. I continue to be asked if people can do *Professional Foul* on stage. There are two different possibilities. One is that somebody says, 'Can I do *Albert's Bridge*? on the stage,' and you say, 'There it is, do your best, it's not written for the stage, but that's your problem.' With other things like *Professional Foul*, I wouldn't have it done unless I personally adapted it for the stage. I don't particularly want to do it. I don't know whether I can do it.

MG: Why did you write that originally for television rather than for the stage? Was it a commission?

TS: Yes.

MG: Having seen it, I could imagine it in the theatre.

TS: I'm not sure. It's got scenes in the passenger section of an airplane, a hotel lobby, a lift, a hotel corridor. It could be one of these abstract stage plays with no set. Then what you've got is a television play on stage. Also it's only 80 minutes long. And there's a scene which is a lecture to the audience.

MG: Part of the reason for my suggesting it is that I saw David Hare's *A Map of the World* last night. It's not so far removed.

TS: I wrote David a longish letter when I saw it. I said it was a superb argument play, and the woman is unplayable. I then tore my letter up and sent him a postcard, which was two sentences, saying how much I liked what I liked. And he wrote back saying what a tactful postcard and he realised there were problems but he thinks he can solve them. And that was that. The storytelling aspect of most plays is often full of problems. But as a writer of dialogue, of sentences, of thoughts, he's just the best.

I'm the world's best audience. I assume what I see is exactly what everybody meant me to see, and there's a reason for everything . . . The end of my story is that David wrote back to me, saying, 'I saw your play. I liked it so much, but I didn't write you because I didn't know what to say about its structural problems.'

MG: Back to radio plays. You don't feel you're wasting material?

TS: No. I hesitate because in *The Dog It Was That Died* I used up an idea, which I had been thinking about for a stage play, about someone who can't remember which side he has been recruited by. It could have been the kernel of a full-length play with other things in it. I never did it or knew how to do it, so I don't regret that I've now used it.

MG: But you could use it again.

TS: Yes. Bits of *Travesties* I stole from myself, changed from the radio play *Artist Descending a Staircase* . . . That idea I used for a radio play: I always thought of it being about a man who wakes up after some sort of accident and has amnesia, and is enlisted by both sides, each claiming that he works for them. I didn't like this, but I couldn't think of what else to do. He must have lost his memory, otherwise there's no play. But while writing it, I discovered that it was no problem at all. He didn't have amnesia; he just forgot.

MG: In the test for astronauts, one of the questions is, have you ever had amnesia, and the best answer is, 'I don't remember,' which sounds like a line out of one of your plays.

TS: It's like that thing in Parkinson's Law. How do you choose a successful candidate for a job? The admiralty has a system where if there are three candidates, the admiral would say, 'What was the number of the taxi you came in?' And the guy who said, 'I came by bus', was thrown out. The guy who said, 'I didn't notice', was thrown out. The guy who lied, '4736250', got the job.

MG: I find it curious that your plays have not been filmed.

TS: The only play that seemed to be a possible film was *Night and Day*. I wrote a draft, which of course jealously guarded the play. It wasn't really a very good movie script, it was the play slightly loosened up. A friend of mine, a film director, pointed this out. It didn't need much pointing out. When enough time had passed, I didn't feel so protective about the play, so I did it again, and I just treated it rather brutally. The result was a much more successful script. It might still be done. Part of what's good about *Travesties* and *Jumpers* is the fact that they're happening in the practical physical limitations of the stage. In a medium where you can do anything you like, the theatricality of the play counts for practically nothing. Your conscious enjoyment of a pyramid of acrobats – so what? Also, of course, whenever the subject comes up, my notorious verbosity is always invoked as the reason why my plays are not made into movies. A guy last

51

week told me he tried to get somebody interested in *The Real Thing*, and he was told it just wasn't movie material. It wasn't that it was too many words, it was too many ideas. A talk piece.

MG: Of all the media you work in, you do enjoy the stage the most?

TS: It's a kind of snobbery. I think of the stage as being real playwriting. It's completely irrational. Radio is probably more real playwriting because you just have the actor's voice and the words you wrote. On-stage you have the director to control the images.

MG: In *The Real Thing*, you talk about Desert Island Discs. Could you talk about Desert Island Books, Plays, People? What play would you take to a desert island?

TS: Just to read?

MG: It could be staged.

TS: When you do the programme, you're given a long time to think about it. It's a very important question. The trouble is almost everything seems not quite enough.

MG: And Desert Island Books?

TS: I'd be tempted to say *Finnegans Wake*, just to pass the time, but I'm not sure if I would really like to.

MG: Have you read it?

TS: No, I've just scratched the surface.

MG: I might take Proust.

TS: That's a good idea. I took it on holiday once and got through one and a half volumes. The holiday ended and that was the end of Proust. Tell the truth, I might take a reference book. I love reference books.

MG: People wonder where your thoughts come from.

TS: They don't come out of books. I'm not an academic, you see. When you asked me about books and plays, I was thinking that the trouble with being a practitioner, you know less than the people who criticise and study. Much less. There are probably wonderful Restoration and Jacobean plays that I never read a line of. All I know is what I see.

MG: Your knowledge has come while reading up on a subject?

TS: Yes. In point of fact, on the few occasions I have written on a subject which could be termed specialist, like moral philosophy, or what was happening in Zurich in 1917, most of what I've used is a kind of general background, which one picks up by reading newspapers or talking to people in pubs or whatever. It's not a research job. The research element is a small proportion of it. You get certain anchor facts correct. It might be a date or whatever. But everything which *Jumpers* is about I didn't need to read at all: general questions about relativism, moral absolutes, this is stuff you can get in your bathtub. I started reading books to check out what other people were writing about it. It showed I wasn't being too naive about my own ideas. Also I read books because I enjoy reading them. When I stop enjoying, I stop reading.

MG: In *The Real Inspector Hound*, *Night and Day* and *The Real Thing*, you deal with things you have direct personal knowledge of: criticism, journalism and theatre.

TS: But it's a very playful exhibition of knowledge, isn't it? There's nothing very specialised about it.

MG: But to an outsider it would seem as specialised as *Travesties* and *Jumpers*.

TS: All I can say is, if I hadn't been a journalist, I would have had to do more research for *Night and Day* than I had to do

53

for *Jumpers*. What you need to know for *Jumpers* you don't have to research. I don't even know where you'd go for research.

In August 1983, Stoppard was in New York to work with Mike Nichols casting The Real Thing for Broadway. One afternoon, he and I were scheduled to meet for a drink at the Carlyle Hotel. Stoppard arrived late and looked as if he had just been roused from hibernation. The dialogue went like this:

TS: I dreamed I was on the top floor of the Algonquin with a lot of people including Mike. I couldn't find my bag. I couldn't figure out what to do – and I realised I had fallen asleep again and was supposed to be down here. Well, this is probably the most ill-fated series of interviews. I'm either half asleep or pulled in different directions, as I was when you visited me at my home. When we met at Brown's, I forgot what my excuse was. I sort of sunk to the occasion.

MG: You 'sunk' because it was a hot day and we were sharing a palanquin. I want to read a few lines from your plays and to recall some things you said to me in the past, to see if you still believe them. Here's a line from *Artist Descending a Staircase*: 'Skill without imagination is craftsmanship and gives us many useful objects such as wickerwork picnic baskets. Imagination without skill gives us modern art.'

TS: I believe that.

MG: Which is more important, imagination or skill?

TS: Imagination, because it fulfils your internal life. If you're making a living at it, you'd better have some skill.

MG: Another line from that play: 'How can one justify a work of art to a man with an empty belly?' Your answer was, 'Make it edible.'

TS: That's not an entirely adequate answer, is it? Somebody's on the ropes there. As a matter of fact, I don't think art needs that sort of justification. You can't wait until everybody is fed before you begin art. What happens is that they're hungry and they're starved for art.

MG: In the first of our conversations you said, 'I write plays because writing dialogue is the only respectable way of contradicting myself. I'm the kind of person who embarks on an endless leapfrog down the great moral issues.' Are you still having dialogues with yourself?

TS: Yes, but I'm more opinionated than I used to be. I still like to write arguments. I've always enjoyed scenes where there are two people with bats, banging this ball across a net at each other.

MG: You've said that so many of your characters talked alike – that it was you yourself talking. I would think you might not feel that way any longer.

TS: As a matter of fact I do, I think. I don't think I'm any more now than then a writer who delineates character with great relish and care, and finds a very different voice for different types of people.

MG: Don't you think the two older men in *The Real Thing* are different, or is the difference a result of the actors?

TS: I think it's mainly the actors. I rely on that a lot. I better make this clear, I'm not saying this in any sense as an apology. As long as you don't claim that one of them is the French ambassador and the other one is a coal-miner from South Wales, it doesn't matter that they talk the same. The scene is about what they say, as much as it is about what kind of person is saying it. On the whole, I'm fairly brutal about making these characters say what I want to be said.

MG: Does that mean you would not write an inarticulate character?

TS: I don't think I've written anything where the main characters are inarticulate because my reason for writing about a subject is to say certain things, and somebody has to be there to say them.

MG: In order to qualify as a character in one of your plays, does a person have to have a certain level of articulation?

TS: Exactly. In *Travesties*, I chose to write about three or four people, one of whom was Rumanian, Tristan Tzara. I didn't want to write for a Rumanian. He had too many important things to say for me to say them in broken English. It was a terrific relief when it turned out the whole play could take place inside the head of this old man, this fantasist. The Rumanian could speak like anybody, and he did. He had to speak like a character from *The Importance of Being Earnest*. In *Night and Day*, the African dictator is the only African dictator, so far as I was concerned, who went to the London School of Economics. He had to, because he had to say all the things I wanted him to say.

MG: He had to because he was in your play?

TS: No. He was in my play because he had to say those things.

MG: That reminds me of Shaw, the fact that the working-class characters in his plays, people such as Alfred P. Doolittle, are all so articulate.

TS: I keep hearing about my being in some sense a Shavian playwright, but this is the first time that comment has made any kind of specific sense. That is a common denominator. Doolittle is a dustman but he's an exceptional dustman, because he would have to be in order to say what he has to say.

MG: If you had a dustman in a play, he would have to be . . .

TS: . . . an exceptional dustman. He wouldn't be there to take up the garbage.

MG: Why do you think that's so? Would the unexceptional dustman or African bore you?

TS: It's the other way round, or rather, you're coming in at the wrong intersection. He wouldn't get a chance to bore because I wouldn't be inspired to write about anything that needed to be boring.

MG: When talking about the political effectiveness of art, you said that if you saw something you wanted to change immediately, 'You could hardly do worse than write a play about it.'

TS: 'Hardly do worse' is a bit strong. I still believe that journalism, television journalism particularly, is the most efficient medium for changing the world – in the short term. In the long term, I suppose, the best art has more effect on our moral sensibilities. To talk about a specific case, my wife recently did a television programme about kidney machines. Because there aren't enough kidney machines in England, someone has to make spontaneous moral choices. If you're young or of the professional class, you get one. If you're old or inarticulate, you don't. There's a strange Olympian process going on where a lot of people are told to go away and die.

MG: As you said that, I thought, if someone didn't qualify for a kidney machine, he wouldn't qualify to be a character in a Stoppard play.

TS: That would be a very interesting criterion for choosing characters. That's quite a sharp remark, Gussow. If I were writing a play about the subject, I guess I would be writing about the doctor and maybe a professor of moral philosophy, and someone else would be writing about the dustman needing the kidney machine.

MG: Unless the dustman happened to be Alfred P. Doolittle.

TS: Then he'd be a dustman who would get a kidney machine.

MG: In other respects, you don't feel Shavian?

TS: I didn't say I wasn't. I think they mainly mean a lot of people sitting around discussing something.

MG: And using highfalutin words?

TS: Highfalutin words, but of course Shaw is revived and revived because there's more to it than that. Did you see *Heartbreak House* with Rex Harrison? I was very impressed by him. He's an actor of enormous accomplishment. In his youth, he was a great comedy actor. Then there was this great film star period. It was an interesting reminder that these actors know exactly what they're doing. Harrison never raises his voice but you can hear everything he says.

MG: To return to Shaw, is there something to be said about people from outside England becoming commentators on the English and the English language? On that ground, is there any kinship between you and Shaw?

TS: On the whole, not. I don't think of myself as being particularly interested in Englishness as such. To me, it's just the time and place I live in and the language I use.

MG: How old were you when you came to England?

TS: I was eight. I was at an American school in India.

MG: So you knew English before you went to England?

TS: Oh, English is my language. I wasn't aware of it at the time, but I spoke quite a funny sort of English. English became my first language and Czech my second language when I was five. By the time I got to England, I wasn't speaking Czech at all.

MG: You think of yourself as an Englishman.

TS: Of course. That's where the argument gets fuzzy. I don't think of myself as a foreign writer at all. I became literate in English.

MG: It wasn't like Nabokov moving to other countries and on to America.

TS: No. Because he belonged to the aristocracy, Nabokov spoke English and French when he was a child at home. I think his father was quite fluent in English when Nabokov was a child.

MG: Do you think of him as a model?

TS: I don't. I like him of course. I'm not sure writers think of other writers being models really. If anything, the more you like another writer the more you shy from using him as a model – because you feel the fatal attraction. I was passionate about Hemingway when I started writing, and the first short stories I wrote were bad Hemingway stories. I think he's still my favourite American writer. He got his effects by simple statements. The egregious word in Hemingway is very rare. 'Egregious' is a word he wouldn't have used in his life. He was very self-conscious about writers who used four-syllable words. I think all of his descriptive prose is a miracle. He was like a painter who made you see what he is painting without resorting to any kind of elaboration.

MG: Looking at both you and Pinter, I would have thought that Pinter would fall more naturally in the Hemingway line, and in America, David Mamet.

TS: I asked Harold about Hemingway once, and you're quite right: he shares my admiration of Hemingway, of the short stories, completely.

MG: Could you compare your use of language to his?

TS: You can't leave out subject matter. He wrote about things which young men respond to with a certain thrill. He wrote about exciting and dangerous pursuits.

MG: You haven't written about exciting and dangerous pursuits.

TS: No, but that doesn't mean one doesn't enjoy reading about them. I remember the time I read *Other Voices Other Rooms*, which is a wonderful book, also a dangerous book for a young writer because you can't do it unless you're him. Very rich imagery. It's like being in a tropical jungle, with exotic foliage everywhere. I remember writing a Capote short story in this sort of vein because I just admired the book. One knew that was alien to one's nature. It was just an effect which one tried to reproduce. I read Hemingway next. The fatal thing about Hemingway is that you get the impression that you can reproduce it. For some reason from 17 to 22 I read only American literature. I loved Saroyan. I don't think I would like him so much now. And I read Faulkner and Fitzgerald, but in the end Hemingway was the only American writer whose books I ended up collecting.

MG: Your subject matter, to say nothing of your style, is so dissimilar. He writes about hunting and fishing and winning women and winning wars and being brave, subjects that do not appear with great frequency in your work.

TS: Not with great frequency, no. All I can say to you is, why should one write like what one likes? My enthusiasms are not that narrow. I love Hemingway, but I also love *The Importance of Being Earnest*. I love *Ulysses*.

MG: But your work is a lot closer to Joyce, Nabokov and Wilde than it is to Hemingway and Pinter...Perhaps you're waiting to write a hard-boiled play.

TS: Hard-boiled? I don't know. *Night and Day* was a bit hard-boiled.

MG: I'm not suggesting that you should write like Hemingway. I'm just trying to understand the admiration.

TS: Maybe it's envy for something you can't do.

MG: In *The Real Thing*, the playwright makes a statement about not being able to write about love. Is that you talking about yourself?

TS: It was me talking about myself before writing *The Real Thing*. The play contains self-reference jokes. Henry says when he tries to write a play about love, it comes out 'embarrassing, childish or rude.' The love story, as I wrote it, tries to avoid banality while suggesting it. Henry says in the same scene, 'It makes me nervous to see three-quarters of a page and no *writing* on it. I *talk* better than this.' That's self-reference.

MG: That's the closest you've come to writing about love?

TS: Yes. As far as I'm concerned, this is all I'll do. For better or worse, that's it – the love play! Since then, one or two people have asked me to get involved in writing things about love, 'because he did it in *The Real Thing*.' But it's not like that. You've done that. You can't do it again. I think love is the only area that might be private to a writer.

MG: You've written about sex. *Jumpers*, *Dirty Linen* have erotic moments.

TS: I suppose so, but none of it's private. It's all theatre sex, theatre lust, witty, articulate sex. Love is a very interesting subject to write about. I've been aware of the process that's lasted 25 years, of shedding inhibition about self-revelation. I wouldn't have dreamed of writing about it 10 years ago, but as you get older, you think, who cares?

[At this point, Mike Nichols arrives, and apologises for intruding.]

MG: We've just finished talking about sex. We're on our way to religion.

MN: You've got only country and Yale to go. You might still make it by eight. You don't have to do this in front of me.

TS: It doesn't make any difference. We're talking about my loss of inhibitions. What did I say about God?

MG: 'The idea of God is slightly more plausible than the alternative proposition that, given enough time, some green slime could write Shakespeare's sonnets.'

MN: Would the green slime have to be in the British Museum?

MG: The green slime would *be* the British Museum.

B reezing *into lunch, he was wearing a hunting-style jacket and boots. He looked as if he were headed for the north woods rather than Broadway. Actually he had just come from a rehearsal of* The Real Thing. *I asked him how he would compare Peter Wood and Mike Nichols as directors, and that set him off on a discussion of his method of writing as it relates to direction.*

TS: I don't build from the ground up. I have intuitive ideas, which I don't analyse when I'm writing. Things are coherent – instinctively. A play doesn't have a secret skeleton key, which, if you find it, means you've done it. The English idea of American playmaking is that there's more psychological examination going on, which, I think, is true, broadly speaking.

MG: You've said that bad art is fully thought out: when the artist knows exactly where he's going.

TS: I think a text that leaves no room for any kind of discovery will, in the end, be mechanistic. If you do something mechanistically, then it goes wrong very quickly. It's like a bridge which is absolutely rigid; it has no play in it, no sway in it. It will break the moment the pressure goes wrong. An actor needs to know a great deal about what's under the surface so that the thing doesn't snap the moment you get a syllable wrong or an inflection wrong.

MG: When you're writing a play, are you often surprised by where the play goes?

TS: Yes, quite often. When you write a play, it makes a kind of noise in your head, and you think that's the only noise it can possibly make to be your play. The rehearsal tells you that's not true. The production doesn't have to produce the noise that the play makes in your head when you wrote it – not all the time. To give you a practical example: I quite often write scenes where people have a row. You can do a scene where two people profoundly disagree with each other in a very quiet way, which would be more true than having a row.

MG: I'm still not clear what inspired *The Real Thing* beyond the fact that the first scene was to have been written by someone in the second scene.

TS: It's quite hard to remember. I can only remember two things. One was what you've just said: the same situation recurs a couple of times in different circumstances, so that it's played differently. The other was what I mentioned in England, that public attitudes are a kind of mirror of a private disturbance. People in the play take certain public postures which are connected with what the play calls a private derangement. Half of the impetus for *Night and Day* was to write about love and marriage, and I guess this play went back to that.

MG: Was it a response to people saying that you had not written about love – or were not able to write about it?

TS: No. Not at all. It was just something to write about. I don't have a lot of things to write about, frankly.

MG: That's what you said several years ago, and you still have things to write about.

TS: Well, I suppose it's getting more true all the time. I certainly have no idea or sense of a stage play to follow this one.

MG: I read *Artist Descending a Staircase*. I'd like to see it on stage.

TS: Various people have asked me if they could do a stage version of it, or if I would. But I never wanted to.

MG: Perhaps you can't visualise it.

TS: We were talking about that in rehearsal this morning. You're rehearsing in this three-dimensional space with furniture in it, and you use the space and furniture and doors, and in different ways all that becomes useful, whether you're doing *Othello* or *Death of a Salesman* or whatever. I said, in England all these plays get done on the radio. On one level at least, if you can do *Othello* or *Death of a Salesman* on the radio, that logically presupposes that the dialogue 'works' without a three-dimensional space, without furniture, doors. The answer is: because the audience occupies this three-dimensional space there's a set of expectations about how it's used. I don't mean that people have rules about theatre, it's just that subconsciously a stage play which was presented as a radio play would just seem very static, whereas with a radio play the expectations are defined by the circumstances. You make the adjustment and take it for what it is.

MG: Although a play like *Death of a Salesman* can be effective on radio or on a record, your stage plays, such as *Jumpers* and *Travesties*, might lose their theatricality on radio. On the other hand, *Artist Descending a Staircase* is quintessentially a radio play.

TS: Obviously there are large elements of *Travesties* which you cannot do on radio but there are pages of duologue and for three people where there is none of that visual element. When you have Tzara and Henry Carr sitting in two chairs and talking for two and a half pages, what is it that makes it different from a radio production?

MG: You seem to set obstacles for yourself according to the medium.

TS: When *Rosencrantz* was done on radio, I had to write a new opening for it, which set up what was happening, just to make it possible for radio. I wrote a radio play since *Artist Descending a Staircase: The Dog It Was That Died*. It starts óff with a guy jumping off a bridge onto a barge in the middle of the Thames. I guess you could do that on stage.

MG: Violent death figures prominently in a number of your plays including *Artist Descending a Staircase*.

TS: I suppose that's true. It's also true that I've written plays where it doesn't, haven't I?

MG: Well, Rosencrantz and Guildenstern do die.

TS: *Jumpers* has a tortoise and a hare who die, not to mention a gymnast. I don't think it means anything.

MG: Academics keep writing books parsing your plays for symbols and motifs.

TS: One picks them up with a terrible shudder as if you're the victim of an accident. It's a very uninteresting subject for me. A lot of what can be said about my work is true without its opposite necessarily being false. I started going through one book and skipped to the quotations. I read the bits that are quoted from my plays to see how they sound.

In rehearsal under the pressure of time and anxiety, little bits get left out. Things don't seem to justify themselves in performance.

MG: You habitually revise your plays.

TS: Doesn't everybody?

MG: But when you write a play, it's published and then you make changes and bring out another edition. And then another edition.

TS: That's true. I keep fiddling with them. When Samuel French publishes an acting edition, it will probably be different from the London edition because it will have the

American discoveries. I've also done the opposite, put in stuff which I've then regretted.

MG: And often there's a germ of another play within a play, as with *Artist Descending a Staircase* leading to *Travesties*. A quote from you: 'If it's worth using once it's worth using twice.'

TS: A joke. It's a joke about jokes.

MG: When Beckett said he would use a statement followed by refutation, to you that is the essential Beckett joke; an immediate contradiction.

TS: Yes. There are tiny versions of that in this play.

MG: In *Jumpers*, a vase drops and you hear the sound of a trumpet being kicked downstairs.

TS: A sound pun. It's very difficult to know why things are funny. Vaclav Havel did a thing called *The Anatomy of the Gag*, and it all came down to incongruous juxtaposition. He had examples from Chaplin films, which were only funny because two ordinary things were put together and one thing became amusing. There are certain jokes which have only to do with the substitution of the unexpected word in a familiar context.

One insight into a sort of humour, which has to do with what I think I write: if you translate something into French and then have it translated back into English by somebody who didn't know the original, you'd lose what was funny. If I said to you, 'The necessity of having a job is extremely inconvenient to those of us who like going to pubs', it would be an extremely lame remark. What it is is a very inept translation of my theoretical French edition of Oscar Wilde, the English of which is 'Work is the curse of the drinking classes.' That has entirely to do with manipulating the sentence to remind you of its opposite. It's not a funny *idea*.

MG: That may be the difference between a joke and wit. It becomes witty when it gets closer to the original Wilde.

TS: Having my words transcribed and quoted gives them an emphasis which I don't feel. 'If a thing is worth using once, it's worth using twice.' The problem is that the printer didn't have a typeface to tell you how casual the remark was. In print it has the same weight as all the other remarks, some of which were not casual at all. You don't know the difference.

MG: What sort of people did you interview when you were a journalist?

TS: People like me. I interviewed actors or writers or people who came to Bristol with a show. Sometimes I didn't know enough about them to do it, so you're kind of bluffing. I once wrote down a lot of things Harold Pinter said in public and printed them on my arts page. I didn't interview Pinter. I asked but he wouldn't give me an interview. It was a good piece because he spoke so interestingly.

MG: Did you ever interview Peter O'Toole?

TS: Yes, after I left Bristol. I did a long piece about him in a magazine. He was the most exciting actor I had seen. When he was doing *Hamlet* and I was in the suburbs reporting on a local politician or something, I would betray my employer by leaving before the story was finished to get back before *Hamlet* finished to see him to do one soliloquy. He did Hamlet, Jimmy Porter and Vladimir in *Godot* in the same season. And then ended up in a pantomime.

MG: Was it really O'Toole and *Look Back in Anger* that made you switch to theatre?

TS: No, it was a delayed fuse. That was a couple of years before I started writing a play. That must have been around 1957 or 1958 and I didn't start writing plays until 1960. I was just quite content to be a member of the audience. I liked being a reporter. That's what I wanted to do.

MG: Did you ever regret not going to college?

TS: Yes. Just to have the reading time. I'm self-educated to some extent because I was a very bad pupil at school, and I just read rubbish until I was 19. I remember reading an article by Clive James. He was talking about his school days. They would have to say what they read that summer and all these smartass guys around him would say, *Ulysses* and *Middlemarch*, and Clive would say *Biggles in the Orient*. That was me! I knew nothing about what was worth reading.

MG: You had a lot to catch up with.

TS: Yes, and I still haven't read *Middlemarch*, but don't tell anybody.

MG: Your next play is about *Middlemarch*.

TS: It's about a man who can't read *Middlemarch*.

MG: But you want your children to be educated, don't you?

TS: There's an extremely overprivileged rule in our family, which goes under the maxim, a book is not a toy, which means that they can have any book they like. Literally. As fast as they can read, they can buy another book. That's the Stoppard rule.

MG: Did your self-education begin as a journalist?

TS: Yes. When you ask if I regretted not going to college, there are two sides to that. I do regret it in a way but my last three years in journalism were as valuable in a different sense. I had an extremely secluded adolescence. When you go to a boarding school you don't get to know very much about anything else. Being a journalist is a very good way to get into the deep end of things.

MG: How did you get your first job as a journalist?

TS: I didn't realise how lucky I was until long afterwards. It was a three-paper town, and I got myself an interview with the news editor on one of those papers. They hired two or three people a year, 17-year old boys or girls, paid what used to be called two pounds ten shillings a week. I was living at home. I was just so glad. The last thing that bothered me was getting paid that little. As I said, as an alternative form of education it was very valuable.

MG: But it didn't introduce you to great books, which seems to be a thrust of your later self-education.

TS: It didn't do that. I started reporting when I was 17. I didn't start reading until I was around 20. I had done an enormous amount of reading from the age of five. Like my eldest son, I tend to re-read books I like. There was a book which had an extremely bad effect on me, a famous English humorous book called *England Their England* by a man called A. G. MacDonell, which was published in the thirties. It had a terrible effect on the way I wrote. I wrote like this man for years afterwards. When I got my own column on the newspaper, I was indefatigably facetious. It was good for his book but bad for journalism. I tended to write in a way which demonstrated the writer rather than the subject. If I did an interview, my piece would use the situation to show how well I could do things, how well I could describe the person, not what he said.

Robert Muller, who's married to Billie Whitelaw, used to interview people for the *Daily Mail*. His first sentence would introduce Cliff Richard. Then there would be a large quote and it would go for 1200 words and the quote mark would finish. Muller could have been anybody, and they were a brilliant series of interviews. There wasn't a line in them other than what the person said. I remember thinking this is hopeless. How does one know if Muller is any good? Of course his interviews were much more interesting to read than anything I ever wrote when I interviewed somebody. Megalomania we call it.

I was talking at a college in Maine, and in the bedroom where they put me up there were four books, one of which was *Look Back in Anger*, which I hadn't looked at for fifteen years. I started reading it and it really got to me all over again. I felt really moved and sentimental about my own youth. It brought back all kinds of things. In 1956 I was 19. I remember what my passions and problems were when that play was around. It has the power to evoke all that again. What are the plays we want to see again? N. F. Simpson's *A Resounding Tinkle* and *One Way Pendulum*. I thought they were hysterically funny. I have a soft spot for James Saunders' *Next Time I'll Sing to You*. Wesker's *I'm Talking about Jerusalem* is a play I like too, more than *Roots*. *The Kitchen* ought to be revived.

MG: *Rosencrantz and Guildenstern*?

TS: When people are studying *Hamlet*, they're quite often interested in *Rosencrantz and Guildenstern*.

MG: Riding the coat-tails of *Hamlet*. And *Travesties* rides the coat-tails of *The Importance of Being Earnest*?

TS: Not quite as secure a grasp. With *The Real Thing*, here we are all on our own. No coat-tails!

With a cast headed by Jeremy Irons and Glenn Close, The Real Thing went into rehearsal in New York. Except for several short trips back to England to check up on his television film, 'Squaring the Circle,' Stoppard was at rehearsal every day – on call for explanations and rewrites. He learns about a play by hearing it, and some of the most consequential sections of his plays have been written during rehearsal. At rehearsals, the director and the playwright sat at separate tables, Nichols munching raw vegetables, Stoppard smoking. At the end of the afternoon, the director gave the actors notes; the playwright was quiet but watchful. Changes were small, usually a question of removing Anglicisms. Even as the company was about to leave for Boston, work continued on the play.

Opening in Boston after only a few previews, The Real Thing still needed polishing. There were props in the wrong place, the lighting momentarily failed and actors missed occasional lines. However, the next morning the critic in The Boston Globe extolled everything about the play and the production, calling two of the actors 'perfect' Relaxing over breakfast in his suite at the Ritz, Stoppard was not overwhelmed by the critical reception and explained that there was still work to be done before the play came to New York. As usual, he appeared to be a man very much in balance.

MG: Mike Nichols says you're the only happy writer he knows.

TS: That's an insult. I'm as miserable as anyone – sometimes.

MG: What are you miserable about?

TS: Domestic things. Not worldly matters.

MG: Does your unhappiness extend to your work?

TS: I have black periods, when I promise to deliver something and nothing happens . . . I'm not really a very exploratory writer. I don't pick up a pen and see how things will go. By the time I pick up a pen, I've gone through so much work. Once I have the vague idea of a structure, landmark moments occur which fit into the structure. I have an idea of how a scene will end, but I don't know how to get there. In *The Real Thing*, one of the stimuli has to do with the situation being repeated three times. That gave me two landmarks to head for. One of the comforting things about being a playwright is that a full-length play is not many words. If you run them all together and take out the stage directions, it's 90 pages at the outside. That's a short story.

MG: Mike says you love rehearsals.

TS: I'm happy in Boston, compared to New York. On tour is like being on a raft. You only know each other. You become a gang of people on a raft. There's a wonderful phrase in *Scoop*: The staff at a country house eat 'ruminative feasts'. On tour with actors one has ruminative feasts . . . [Quoting lines from the play.] 'Happiness is equilibrium. Shift your weight.' Shift your weight. That's quite sound. [He stands up and demonstrates, moving from foot to foot.] Equilibrium is pragmatic. You have to get everything into proportion. You compensate, rebalance yourself so that you maintain your angle to your world. When the world shifts, you shift.

December 1994

'The sci and the phys are a phase, like delinquency, which one goes through'

S*toppard was on the brink of a very busy season.* Hapgood, *in its new version, was opening the following evening at Lincoln Center, in a production starring Stockard Channing. That was to be followed several months later by* Arcadia *on the main stage at Lincoln Center's theatre.* Arcadia *was a continuing success in London, and in February* Indian Ink, *his stage version of his radio play,* In the Native State, *was scheduled to open in the West End.*

Arcadia *is one of his most ambitious and most satisfying plays, a prismatic exploration of English history, horticulture, the chaos theory and the difference between the classical and romantic traditions. In the subtext are such issues as the pursuit of epiphany and the nature of genius. Along the way, people keep leaping to the wrong conclusions, which heightens the hilarity and the complexity. One of the many mysteries is who did what to whom in the game room or, rather, the game book, where Lord Byron, as a guest in this elegant country house, is recorded as having shot a hare. At the centre of the play is an historian, Hannah Jarvis, but she is only one of a houseful of kaleidoscopic characters that emerge from the playwright's fervid imagination.*

In contrast to Arcadia, *Hapgood had not been a critical success in its original production in London (in 1988). Since then, Stoppard had revised the play and clarified the plot. This devious comedy-mystery equates the wave-particle theory of light with the double-dealing world of espionage. The new version is twenty minutes shorter and clues the audience earlier that the spy named Ridley might have a double. In this Rubik cube of a play, there are triple, perhaps even quadruple agents and a multiplicity of secret identities.*

After sudden shifts in his busy schedule, the peripatetic playwright was in a suite in a New York hotel, prepared for a long conversation. He lit the first of many cigarettes. His body was reasonably at rest, his mind restlessly in motion.

MG: I thought *Hapgood* was clear the first time I saw it, but I gather many people didn't agree.

TS: Well, it was obviously written for you the first time. I think you were in the minority.

MG: Jack O'Brien's production here [in New York] is very different from Peter Wood's in London.

TS: It's the first different one I've seen. We did it similarly in Los Angeles and then there was a San Francisco production which was based on the British one. The idea this time was to do an American *Hapgood* with American actors, and not bring any baggage from the old one.

MG: You've said, 'If there's a central idea in the play, it is the proposition that in each of our characters is the working majority of a dual personality, part of which is always there in a submerged state.'

TS: That was the hypothesis which generated the play itself, that the dual nature of light works for people as well as things, and the one you meet in public is simply the working majority of that person. It's a conceit. It may have some truth to it.

MG: And the dual personality doesn't refer simply to counter-spies, but to Hapgood herself and others.

TS: It's not really dual personality. It's just that one chooses to 'be' one part of oneself, and not another part of oneself. One has a public self and a submerged self. It's that sort of duality.

MG: Is one real, the other false?

TS: No, they're both part of the whole person.

MG: Does that mean that Hapgood's 'sister' is as real as Hapgood herself?

TS: What it is inclined to mean is that circumstances lead her to take on what she would initially think of as a false personality, but in doing so she discovers that she is using part of herself that she simply hasn't used but has no difficulty in expressing, in assuming. So the woman who wouldn't touch Ridley with a bargepole begins to fancy him in a different set of coordinates. The woman who rather disdains him begins to find him sympathetic. These two arcs intersect at the moment where she kills him, where the working majority of Hapgood pulls the trigger. It all seems to be part of my Master Plan. But one fumbles one's way towards these things, you understand.

MG: The working majority pulls the trigger, but the secret recessive minority can sleep with Ridley.

TS: And grieves. Yes.

MG: And we all have this in our personalities.

TS: Kerner [a Russian double agent] claims so. He says to Blair [Hapgood's superior officer], 'Well, here you are, bachelor of arts, first class, and yet you insist on laboratory standards for reality, whereas I the scientist insist on its artfulness.' It's that kind of contradiction which makes up the whole person.

MG: And it's something other than multiple personalities.

TS: It's not multiple personalities. It's a complex personality only part of which runs the show.

MG: Is that true in your life as well?

TS: Well, I wouldn't have the presumption to exempt myself [laugh] from this general rule.

MG: When you were a journalist, you operated both as a critic and as an interviewer, and you used different names.

TS: I did, only because it seemed a bit second-rate to write too many things on the same page. It wasn't that I was trying to conceal half of myself. But the thesis is really to do with people's temperaments. Their personal histories, like my personal history, is not central to the idea at all – the fact that I was born into one language and grew up in another, and so on. That doesn't sound irrelevant by any means, but it's not supposed to be a comment about that kind of life, about my kind of life. It's supposed to be a comment about any person who is born in New York, lives in New York, dies in New York, but nevertheless cannot be construed like a simple sentence.

MG: Explain that further.

TS: I'll go on from 'nevertheless' then. It cannot be unlocked with one key. One of the suspicious things about my thesis (which in a sense you have insisted on): it's not something I feel like sounding off about, page after page. It's a curiosity, which intrigues me. The suspicious thing about it may be that it's a key that opens any lock. You can apply it, as you just applied it, to people whose life is changed circumstantially. The audience here, more than previously, pick up on what you and I have just been talking about, quite considerably. I noticed last night, when Kerner is telling Hapgood about electrons, you can see the penny drop for her when she says, 'It's its own alibi.' The play's a melodrama, however. One keeps speaking of thesis and hypothesis and so on. But it's a new-fashioned melodrama, isn't it?

MG: It certainly has to work on that level for the audience to tune in to it.

TS: It's always been true of this play. You can tell the audience that they're about to witness a con trick, but they get sucked in to the con-man's point of view. You tell them, we're going to tell lies to Ridley. Then you set up a scene where everything is being done for Ridley's sake, and it's a lie. But the audience seem equally surprised when the rug is pulled out from under him. They've gone along with it, although one has told them we're going to do it.

MG: You keep the audience wondering: could be this a triple or even a quadruple agent?

TS: It might be another corner.

MG: Could you ever be a spy?

TS: No, I shouldn't think so. Hapgood says she makes a good living telling lies. I don't think I could do that. I'm not good at it. I'm rather a slipshod careless person. I'm not methodical.

MG: Perhaps that's the best kind of spy, someone who would seem to be slipshod.

TS: I think that's the one that gets caught. I could be a spy, but not for very long.

MG: Thinking about Hapgood, I wondered if your mother were ever a spy.

TS: Nooo, not that I'm aware of.

MG: At the end of the play, Hapgood is cheering her son on in a game of rugby as his father silently watches. Suddenly I remembered the scene at the end of [the radio play] *Where Are They Now?*, with Gale playing a game and 'the voices distant and almost snatched away by the wind, it is a day he has forgotten but clearly he was very happy.'

81

TS: Yes. Yes.

MG: Which I suppose is as close to the autobiographical bone as anything you've written. Do you feel the similarity of images there?

TS: I do, yes. It's partly using what one has. I have four sons who played rugby at prep school. So there's that. That *Where Are They Now* play, it wasn't in any way autobiographical but of course it pillaged my own childhood.

MG: And that image is a happy moment?

TS: It's not something that happened to me, if that's what you mean. I think I've had analogous moments. I remember one, which actually I told Ken Tynan about and he put in that New Yorker profile. I was about seven. I was at school in India, and I remember walking along a corridor, suddenly being overtaken by a great sense of everything being all right, or nothing being wrong. About four, five years ago, I went back to India for the first time and . . . the corridor was still there [laughs].

MG: Were there echoes in the corridor?

TS: Yes. It was strange. It was the corridor to the playground in this school I was at in Darjeeling.

MG: Does that mean that one's happiest memories go back to childhood and to sports?

TS: I don't think there's a general rule about that. Everybody's different. My happiest memories are all kinds. Not really sport, by the way.

MG: An academic could write a thesis about the sporting motifs in your work.

TS: I don't think of my life as a well into which I drop my bucket with a sense of going deeply into myself.

MG: But all the plays have an element of autobiography.

TS: I wonder. Perhaps it's something which it's impossible to escape, and one shouldn't protest against it, though I wouldn't have thought *Rosencrantz and Guildenstern* had anything autobiographical in it. I'm not really the right kind of writer to oblige such a speculation because the area in which I feed off myself is really much more to do with thoughts I have had rather than days I have lived.

MG: A number of misconceptions have sprung up about you and your work, that your plays are divorced from your own life; also that you're very intellectual and unemotional. One certainly doesn't feel that in the scene in which Hapgood is so moved that she cries.

TS: What you're saying is that my working majority is mostly what's perceived and written up.

MG: But there is another side to you.

TS: Yes, absolutely. That particular duality has become a bit of a cliché about me. It's rather a high-tech production of *Hapgood*, so it does encourage that view of the work.

MG: But there is a heart there.

TS: I don't think you would bother to write about it if was about robots. It's only interesting because they're human beings.

MG: In searching for the arc of your career, I made a list of the principal subjects in the plays: *Rosencrantz and Guilden-stern*, theatre-philosophy; *The Real Inspector Hound*, theatre-journalism; *Travesties*, lit-phil; *Jumpers*, phil-gym; *Dirty Linen*, pol-sex; *Night and Day*, journ-pol; *Every Good Boy Deserves Favour*, music-pol; *Cahoot's Macbeth*, theatre-pol;

The Real Thing, theatre-love; *Hapgood*, sci-spy; *Arcadia*, lit-math-hort-arch; *Indian Ink*, lit-art-pol-soc. It seems that the plays are becoming more inclusive or expansive.

TS: And yet *Indian Ink*, or *In the Native State*, is actually a very intimate play. It's a play of intimate scenes. There's something working against the notion that the plays are expanding in their horizons . . . There is a lot of lit in the plays and a lot of phil, which I think is fair comment on what I'm made up of.

MG: A lot of lit and phil and more and more sci and phys.

TS: I've got a funny feeling the sci and phys are a phase, like delinquency, which one goes through.

MG: It's lasted two plays.

TS: Exactly, it's two plays. Two suggests purpose, misleadingly.

MG: One is singular, two is a coincidence, three is a trend.

TS: In the case of those two plays, they began because I stubbed my toe against two pieces of information or two areas of science which I found really interested me. It didn't seem to be a release of some scientist within me. On the contrary, it seemed to be going against what really interests me, what I choose to read, and so on. I thought that quantum mechanics and chaos mathematics suggested themselves as quite interesting and powerful metaphors for human behaviour, not just behaviour, but about the way, in the latter case, in which it suggested a determined life, a life ruled by determinism, and a life which is subject simply to random causes and effects. Those two ideas about life were not irreconcilable. Chaos mathematics is precisely to do with the unpredictability of determinism. Hifalutin words, but it's actually a very fascinating door, a view through a cracked-open door. Pinning myself down to your question: I have no sense of looking for a third such fascinating scientific metaphor, and I have no reason to suppose that I'll stub my toe on a third one.

MG: How did you stub your toe against those two?

TS: Casually.

MG: Books in an airport?

TS: I joke like that, but it's not one book on one day. My life is sectioned off into hot flushes, pursuits of this or that. Rather in the same way as a year ago or more, a fairly quiescent interest in or sympathy towards Roman poetry and literature of antiquity suddenly had its turn. I think it turned into something more obsessive through reading about A. E. Housman, again somebody whom I had read for years on and off. That was another quiescent interest.

MG: Because you collect books for specific projects, I have this picture of an enormous library with tall bookcases in sections.

TS: It is rather like that, but unfortunately it's in different houses. A lot of it is in Iver and a lot of it is in Chelsea, and some in storage. Odd that you should say so, I was looking at a rather beautiful and expensive library ladder last week.

MG: And you read most of those books?

TS: Yes.

MG: Do you read Latin?

TS: I can't say I read Latin. I studied Latin up to what in England we call A level. So it's not gibberish to me. But I read it with cribs. What I enjoy is reading a particular poem or a poet in numerous translations, to see how different translators try to find the original. There's a play to be written about translation, I think. There's one ode by Horace that's been translated so many times that there's actually a wonderful book which consists entirely of translations of this single ode.

85

MG: That leads me to think of your translations.

TS: As you know, in the theatre, the word translation covers a multitude of venal sins. Life being life, most of the people who are brilliant at Polish are not good at writing dialogue, and most people who are good at writing English dialogue are not good at Polish or Hungarian or German. It tends to be a two-man or two-woman job even when these people don't work together, and sometimes never even meet.

MG: Do you always work from a literal translation?

TS: Yes. I've done two Schnitzlers, a Nestroy and a Molnár, and I worked on a Lorca. It doesn't feel like much over 30 years. Years and years and years ago, one of my resolutions – now a failed resolution – was to learn a language well enough, Russian by choice, not simply for purposes of translation but so that I could read things the way they were meant to be understood.

MG: And what have you done about that?

TS: Nothing. I postponed reading *War and Peace* until I could read Russian. The result is now I cannot read Russian and I have not read *War and Peace*. Clive James, who is an old friend of mine, learned Russian because he wanted to read Pushkin. He learned Russian and read Pushkin, as did Edmund Wilson.

MG: Late in life, I.F. Stone learned Greek.

TS: It was a good book, *Trials of Socrates*. I did read Greek until I was 17, but for some reason I have never been as interested by Greek literature as by Latin, though in fact one of the things on my little list was always to look at Aristophanes because it always irritated me how unfunny Aristophanes is in English. I thought there must be a way to make it really funny. But I decided to learn Greek properly first, so I never got around to that. Aristophanes and *War and Peace* may be my deathbedside books, if that's a word.

MG: Perhaps you need a long sabbatical.

TS: I don't know about these sabbaticals. My ambition is to retire, and has been for ages. When I say retire I mean just placidly writing at my own speed without owing anything to anybody, without anybody waiting for what I'm writing. I never seem to manage to do that. I think it's a temperamental defect; that's pretty clear by now.

MG: If that really is your objective, you're going about it in entirely the wrong way.

TS: I am. I tend to get overcommitted, partly because things always take me longer than I think they will.

MG: You've said that you prefer it when you have only one thing on your plate at a time, and now your plate would fill this table.

TS: One isn't entirely in control of these things. I wrote a film script of *Hopeful Monsters* by Nicholas Mosley a year ago, and ever since then I was waiting for the next stage to happen. And sometimes the next stage never does happen: finding a director who's keen to do it, and all that. Now that's happened with *Hopeful Monsters*, but it could have happened six months ago, or it could have never happened, or it could have happened six months from now. But it turned out to happen when I'm going into rehearsal with *Indian Ink*, so it's not good for either.

MG: What is the status of the movie of *Cats*? You've completed the screenplay?

TS: *Cats* is a very long-term project because animation takes a very long time. But I've done *Cats*, and undoubtedly, as people work on it, there will be alterations to it.

MG: Why did you write the screenplay for *Cats*?

TS: I was asked to do it a long time ago at a meeting with

Steven [Spielberg] and Andrew [Lloyd Webber]. I felt a bit out of place. I didn't quite see what I was supposed to bring to it. I just gently backed away from it. It must have been nearly two years ago that Trevor [Nunn] took me to lunch and asked me if I would do it. I said I have already been asked and didn't really know what to do. I said I'd go and see it again. I really like working with Trevor very much, and decided to have a go at it. At that point, it wasn't exactly Steven's film. He's come back since then. I suppose it was really Andrew, Trevor and I working together to prepare something which they then wanted to take to a film company, in this case Universal. Between my first encounter with *Cats* and my lunch with Trevor, the whole thing had come back into Andrew's life. It was like a new start. Your question was why did I want to do it? Firstly, I liked the poems.

MG: Did you like the music?

TS: Yes. I'm not a tremendous enthusiast of musicals. I don't often go to see them, to be honest. I mean I've been working with Trevor for years, but I've never seen *Les Miserables*. I have been to his office a hundred times, with *Les Miserables* outside the window where Trevor can look at the queue. And I never got round to seeing it. I'm not sure if he knows that. I'm not doing the film of *Cats because* it's a musical. That's really not an area of expertise for me at all. But it's the kind of job that's quite interesting. There was a vestige of a plot, the beginning of a plot, a faintly discernible tendency towards having a plot. But after I saw the musical, I had no recollection of what that little plot was supposed to be. It didn't seem that important to the evening. It was more like a concert musical, a concert with dance.

There was a kidnap in it, which I had entirely forgotten, and the truth is I had forgotten it because it doesn't really matter. It wasn't really what you were there for. You were there for the music, the Eliot and the production. Actually the job was a puzzle problem. Here are these elements, here are these characters, invent a story with the songs in the following order. As it turned out, Andrew fortunately didn't hold to having the songs in a particular order, which had been his first feeling about the way the show should be structured. I couldn't really see how the songs could stay in that order. Also, there was a lot of discussion about which songs had to be omitted because an animated film is a lot shorter than a stage musical. An animated film is a very short number. Ninety minutes is long. Eighty-five minutes is better, so one couldn't use all the songs.

It's one of the few collaborations I've enjoyed. I like working with myself usually. But because of the songs and the music, I couldn't work by myself. I had to sell Andrew and Trevor on the advisability of changing the order of the songs. It all ended up quite happily, and artists are drawing away, but that doesn't mean it's my screenplay they are drawing.

MG: You're not interested in musicals, but you like music.

TS: I like music. I like pop music, certain kinds of jazz. There's no music that I dislike, but there's very little music I listen to with any degree of understanding or recognition. You know, Miriam is a great opera fan. I used to go to lots of operas with her. I would say, 'Have I seen this one?' 'Of course you have.' I would say 'What did it look like?' I'd remember them visually, not aurally. I'd remember the one that had a crosshatch design by David Hockney. I'm really a shameful object when it comes to 'proper music'.

MG: Have you seen all of Lloyd Webber's shows?

TS: I've seen *Starlight* and *Sunset* and *Cats*, but I've never seen *Phantom of the Opera*. Because you know it's always there, one is always going to see something else which might close. You feel that *Phantom* is there, like the Eiffel Tower. There's no rush.

MG: To return to *Arcadia*, where did it begin? With the book, *Chaos*?

TS: I think so. On the other hand, I must have been reading

89

Chaos because of something else I read, maybe in a magazine or a newspaper. It's like a river with more than one source. There's no 'where' about it. You just mentioned the Chaos mathematics book. At the same time, I was thinking about Romanticism and Classicism as opposites in style, taste, temperament, art. I remember talking to a friend of mine, looking at his bookshelves, saying there's a play, isn't there, about the way that retrospectively one looks at poetry, painting, gardening, and speaks of classical periods and the romantic revolution, and so on. Particularly when one starts dividing people up into classical temperaments and romantic temperaments – and I suppose it's not that far from *Hapgood* in a way. The romantic temperament has a classical person wildly signalling, and vice versa.

You and I tend to talk about all this as if it really works like that, as if there's this acorn that you find somewhere and put manure around, and water, and hope it grows into some kind of sapling, and so on and so forth. It doesn't seem to me to be that kind of orderly natural development.

MG: No single acorn?

TS: It's more than that. I have the feeling that you throw the acorn away at some point. I talk about, or you encourage me to talk about, a book or a thought which generates everything that follows. It's true in a limited sense, but an alternative way of making a picture of the process would be to say that it's something that starts you up, like a motor gets started up, like a cranking handle. Then you throw the handle away, and drive off down the road somewhere and see where the road goes.

MG: Was *King Lear* the acorn of *Rosencrantz and Guildenstern*?

TS: No. The real beginning of that had very much to do with having these two outsiders knocking about the court and not understanding what was happening. Goodness knows why I thought that, but there we are.

MG: What's an acorn that you've discarded?

TS: When it comes to it, I don't think *Arcadia* says very much about these two sides of the human personality or temperament. I don't think it's in the play. It's by no means in the foreground. And yet, it's firing all around the target, making a pattern around the target.

MG: Where does the texture start? Suddenly horticulture enters, and then Lord Byron. You didn't set out to write a play about horticulture and Byron?

TS: No, I didn't, but I had read one or two books about Byron over the years, and I was reading them with a faint sense of undisclosed purpose. I suppose if you're my kind of writer you're always working. One's leisure reading is subconsciously purposeful. There are very few things I read that clearly have no future in my work [pause]. Is that true? I'm reading *A Suitable Boy*, a 1500-page novel, and I probably began it long after I needed it. I think I had written the first Indian play before *A Suitable Boy* was even published. I trawled it in as part of my Indian library and found that I just enjoyed it so much, I've been reading it every now and again, long after I had any ostensible use for it.

MG: But something might come out of it?

TS: I doubt it. One can't say 'wouldn't', but that's not part of why I'm reading it.

MG: Takes a lot of time to read it.

TS: The way I read it, I do twenty pages before I go to sleep. That's a lot of days there. When it came out in paperback, it came out in three volumes, which made life easier. So I now have volume three next door.

MG: Do you travel with many books?

TS: Usually I do. I've even got a wonderful piece of luggage, which is a travelling bookcase. It's about as big as a bread-bin. I had it on my last trip to New York, but I wanted to come just with hand baggage this time. More than twenty years ago, Miriam was at the carousel at Heathrow, or some-where, and this leather box came round, and when the guy claimed it, she asked him what it was. He showed her, and it was this bookcase, which he got from T. Anthony [a New York luggage store], and in no time I had a travelling book-case. For twenty years I've gone on holiday and roundabout with this wonderful box. The front comes down, so when you arrive in your hotel room, you have a bookshelf, and there's a pocket in the lid for pens and pencils and things. And you have this row of maybe twelve books. People ask where it came from.

Then T. Anthony stopped making them. I remember they cost $365. It struck me that it was interesting it was a dollar for each day of the year. If you earned a dollar a day, it would take a year to earn this T. Anthony Park Avenue bookcase. A friend of mine in Los Angeles said, 'How do you get this?' I said, 'Oh, they don't make them anymore.' A few weeks later, she sent me a magazine article about a woman who makes luggage. So I called her up and said, 'If I sent you my T. Anthony bookcase, would you be able to make it?' She said, 'I expect so.' The result is I've now had three from her. Perfect, even better, absolutely the way they used to be. I've given one as a wedding present, one as a Christmas present, a third one is about to be given as a Christmas present. My original one is just getting slightly loose in the hinges. I'm now seriously considering having her make me a new one.

MG: You could always use that as an alternate profession.

TS: I could be a luggage broker. On commission. I'd be the agent. I wouldn't have to work in leather.

MG: What books did you bring with you the last time you travelled with your bookcase?

TS: It's partly to do with work. If I bring work with me,

sometimes I have some books. It was three weeks ago. I was finishing *Cats*, so I had scripts in it. And one of the books I happened to be reading at the time. *A Suitable Boy* would certainly be in there. My copy of *Hopeful Monsters*. And a couple of ancillary books. When you're working on a play, you tend to have the mornings free. From lunchtime onwards, you pick up on the previous day's work once you're in previews, and then you work until midnight, if you can call it work. But when you're rehearsing, you have your evenings free. I like work. I haven't seen a play or a film since I've been here.

MG: You still write in longhand and then dictate it into a tape recorder?

TS: Yes. I do exactly that with new work, but when I'm rewriting or changing things, I now prefer to give my secretary lots and lots of pages of longhand with arrows and squiggles, 'insert here'. I love working on a typescript. I love the power of the blue pencil. 'This is rubbish, take it out. Put this in. Turn it around.'

MG: Until I saw *Hapgood* again, I didn't realise that Ridley's first name is Ernest.

TS: I had forgotten that until the other night.

MG: Is that a reference to *The Importance of Being Earnest*?

TS: No, not at all. Goodness knows what I was thinking of. Naming characters is a strange thing. I never felt the person Mrs. Swan married in *In the Native State* had the right name. And his name was . . . I've forgotten what his name was in the radio play. But I always felt there was something wrong with that name. When I was doing *Indian Ink*, I realised his name was Eric. He's now Eric.

MG: Why Hapgood?

TS: I don't know. I wasn't aware that the Archbishop of York was called Habgood, with a B. I just arrived at it. Happy and Good, perhaps. Or Happenstance. Perhapsgood.

MG: And Bernard Nightingale [in *Arcadia*] is named after Benedict Nightingale [the drama critic of the London Times]?

TS: There's this moment where she says, 'I'll give you another name, perhaps another bird: Peacock.' I was looking for a bird name. I'm afraid nobody was further from my mind than Benedict.

MG: Tynan's name was Peacock.

TS: Yes, that's true. That hadn't occurred to me either.

MG: Nightingale's an unusual name.

TS: No, not really. Well, not that unusual. The odd thing about these names is that they kind of detonate in a way that looks pre-planned. In *Arcadia*, Hannah makes reference to Thomas Love Peacock. She believes Bernard's called Peacock, and she says, 'Your illustrious namesake.' He says, 'Florence?' If I'd called him Thrush, God knows what he would have replied. There's a wonderful element of good luck in these things.

MG: You would have thought of some joke about Thrush.

TS: I suppose I would have had to. There's something about the corpse in *The Real Inspector Hound*, the first string critic. I think he's called Duncan. In some way this paid off much much later, with a reference to the dead king in *Macbeth*. This may not be true. Something like this happens in more than one of my plays, and it looks embarrassingly calculated, but so far as I was concerned, it was a complete accident.

MG: Has the Boot and Moon cycle ended?

TS: Seems to. It would be too knowing to do it now because it's been spotted too many times. There's always a Chamberlain in my plays, as you know, because my secretary used to be Chamberlain. She's remarried since then. In the days when she typed my plays off the tape, I used to think, oh I'll wake her up by putting in Chamberlain. I think almost every play has a Chamberlain in it, including *Indian Ink* and *Hapgood*. Is there one in *Arcadia*? I don't mean a character in a play, I mean a reference.

MG: Like Al Hirschfeld putting Ninas into his drawings?

TS: Yes, yes. Now you've got me really worried. Is there a Chamberlain in *Arcadia*?

MG: There is probably an academic who is analysing the motif of Chamberlains in your work. This reminds me: one of the best moments in *Arcadia* is when the girl draws the portrait of the hermit on the landscape, and years later this becomes the sole 'proof' that the hermit existed. Someday someone will go back and write a thesis about the meaning of the Chamberlains.

TS: I'm counting on it.

MG: Tell me about the PEN meeting in Prague.

TS: I only got there for a discussion with Havel, Ronald Harwood and Arthur Miller.

MG: You told me it was a moral dilemma whether you would go to Prague or to New York for the first preview of *Hapgood*.

TS: I sent Jack [Jack O'Brien, director of *Hapgood*] a fax of Havel's letter and said I had a very serious moral dilemma. 'I feel I should go to Prague and miss the first preview. I'm really sorry.' Then Jack was on my answerphone saying, 'Thank God, what a relief, go to Prague, we don't want you here.' So they could do their first preview without The Author Watching. It never occurred to me that The Author Watching was an intimidating idea. They were vastly relieved. I showed up for the second preview, and it was fine.

MG: Is it a *canard* that you're a conservative?

TS: Would it be one? I always thought of myself as a conservative not in a sort of ideological way. I'm really a bit of a failure talking about politics because I never get into the subject or issues in the manner in which a responsible citizen really ought to. I respond in some other way, aesthetically even, certainly emotionally. Emotionally I like to conserve. I don't like impulsive change. But what I like and don't like certainly doesn't divide up into things that the Conservative Party or the Labour Party does. One of the things I hated most of all was when they redrew the country boundaries in England. I grew up with this map of England, where there was the North Riding of Yorkshire and a county called Rutland and there were Somerset and Gloucestershire, and when the Conservatives brought in these newfangled bureaucratic entities called Avon and Cleveland, I was appalled. So my conservatism is trivial in some ways.

I was very pleased with Mrs. Thatcher at the beginning. I thought of her as being a subversive influence, which I found very welcome. The Wilson-Callaghan pre-Thatcher years in English politics I thought were nauseating. I thought politicians had become people one didn't bother to listen to because they seemed desperately anxious not to expose their flanks to any side. There were very few unqualified statements of intent. I loved the way she came in. I was very personally interested in the whole saga of print unions, for example, a huge corrupt scandal which government after government wouldn't tackle.

Which brings us to Murdoch as well. I think he's a very bad influence on English, or indeed global, cultural life. Ten years ago, he was a sort of hero for me, for sending the printers packing. The printers were making newspapers into an impossible economic proposition, and I love newspapers. I was delighted when Murdoch came in in his Australian underhanded way with a lot of money behind him and just destroyed them. It was well overdue. Obviously I was thinking collectively – the print union.

MG: A lot of printers were out of work.

TS: Exactly. I was coming to that very point. This is the difficulty of any pronouncement on an issue. There's a collective, and then there's a personal individual life there. That's why these questions are never quite resolved.

MG: You've been so strong on human rights. What about human rights for printers?

TS: I don't think you have a human right to cheat and steal. There were printers signing on as Mickey Mouse. I just think they pushed their luck. Murdoch said, it's not a union, it's a protection racket. I think that was probably quite fair.

MG: But then you turned against Murdoch.

TS: That's part of a whole shift of feeling about the press as a whole. *Night and Day* contains statements which are still flourished. I read one last week by people who want to leave the press completely untrammelled. I don't know what I want now. I've arrived at a kind of defensive position, which is not entirely where I stand intellectually. I've decided that getting cross about the press is almost like getting cross about the Flat Earth Society. It's become an awful joke. What I find upsetting about the notorious end of the British press is what it says about the readership. I think the tabloid press treat their readers almost as if they are morons. And it's awful the way the readers don't seem to mind.

MG: You said you still like newspapers. Why?

TS: God knows. Here in New York I walk to rehearsal and buy three London papers, yesterday's. I don't know why. Because I grew up with them, I suppose.

MG: You've said, 'Journalism is the last line of defence in this country.'

TS: I think that's still true. I think people would be getting away with much more, were it not for newspapers blowing the whistle, or just being there to observe.

MG: What about newspapers furthering their own agenda, and distorting issues?

TS: It's partly that. But there's a dreadful arrogance about them. This is a banal truism. The tabloids purport to be looking after the public's interest, but if you ever see the face of a news editor when somebody comes in with a story of a politician's sexual escapade, there's no sense there of saving the country from anything or of informing the public of anything important. It's a saturnalia. It's vicious, vindictive, unprincipled and should be beneath the dignity of the profession. It's an ancient, honourable profession, which has fought for its rights, and I don't think it's fought for the right to trade in domestic tribulation. But privacy laws are pretty sinister. I said before that people are still quoting from *Night and Day*. In the Spectator someone was quoting the person in *Night and Day* who said, 'I'm with you on the free press. It's the newspapers I can't stand.'

I once went to a debate on the press, with the editor of the Observer and David Hare on the platform. It must have been the time of *Pravda* [the play by Howard Brenton and Hare that satirised the press]. I was sitting there, a member of the public, and David Hare was attacking the press, and the editor of the Observer was putting up the defence. To my astonishment, the editor then produced a quote from *Night and Day* to back up his case. But I was no longer on his side to that degree. It made me realise that I had shifted. Apart from anything else, *Night and Day* is a work of fiction in which various people argue and put forth points of view. Certainly I stood fairly shoulder to shoulder with the young reporter in the play, when he said the sleazy press is the price you pay for not having somebody with a title and a big blue pencil draw the line.

I'm very unfocused and incoherent on the subject because I'm in the middle of it. For the last year or two I've thought if I can get this properly in focus, I really would like to write another play about journalism. I've shifted to the right here. It's partly because the newspapers are that much worse, partly that I'm that much older and more conservative.

MG: More conservative?

TS: About newspapers. I think I am. I read three newspapers a day as a minimum, five on Sunday, because they educate and inform even yet. I have a thesis about papers at the moment. I'm not sure I have the time or inclination to establish its credentials. It's more an instinct than a thesis. When I was in journalism, there was a kind of divide in the press. There was a knockabout press which quite often was inane and made much of trivial events in public and private life. And then there was another larger body of newspapers, which considered this wasn't really worth the space. My intuition is that the divide in the British press still exists but no longer separates newspaper from newspaper. It goes through the middle of every paper. So you have this astonishing phenomenon now where you get the most dedicated, most highly principled journalism, journalism which does good. It runs campaigns, reports things which need to be reported. Yet jostling about in the same paper are completely silly sort of women's magazine type stories, stories that used to be in TV Times, and fatuous 'exposés'.

I bumped into Andrew Neil [then editor of the Sunday Times] at a party and tried out my thesis on him. He wasn't at all impressed. His view was, 'Yes, but none too soon.' He felt the corruption in English society came from deference. I think he has a mission in life to demonstrate that all deference is bad.

MG: It's also true in America, where gossip gets in the so called serious papers and investigative journalism can be in the tabloids.

TS: Exactly. It's as though the press is now schizoid. When I was a young man going into journalism, there were *newspapers* and there were some odd papers that were hard to

99

classify. They were called *Titbits* and *Reveille*, and they were essentially composed of human interest stories: Siamese twin bites dog kind of stories. And that story has now found its way to the front page of the tabloid Sunday press. The thing that leaves one with a sense of despair is that the newspaper has found its readership and the readership has found its newspaper. To me it looks like a downward spiral into an appalling basement of the subclass, which I would lay at the door of tacky journalism.

MG: I also read many papers, especially in London. I don't know why I do it.

TS: I know why I do it, because I suffer the delusion that my next play but one would be inside this newspaper, and if I don't read it, I won't write the play. Which is a kind of insanity, because I can't read everything. When I'm here I read the New York Times Magazine and am aware that I have not read 51 of the 52. Who knows what was in them?

MG: Do you find the ideas for your plays, other than the ones about journalism, in the newspapers?

TS: Actually, *Arcadia* might have started there. Something must have led me to get hold of Gleick's book [*Chaos*].

MG: Perhaps it was a review of the book.

TS: Good example. I read book reviews for that reason.

MG: Could you imagine having stayed in journalism and not being a playwright?

TS: No. Looking at it now, I would think of that as an unhappy outcome, not because I love the theatre, in quotes, but because it was wonderful to work for myself and not have to be accountable to somebody. It's one of the things we were talking about in Prague. I have a formulation about the luck we've had, which is that people like myself appear to have promoted a recreation into a career. We're getting away with it, and it's the getting away with it part which I don't want to lose. It seems quite capricious, the way one profession is rewarded over another one. There's an evolution in every kind of society, particularly now in what we call the free market society, where certain pursuits are amazingly over-rewarded. Being a popular singer, or in a band. There's no logic in it.

MG: Television journalism as compared to print journalism.

TS: Absolutely. That's an interesting phenomenon. There's a relationship between the face and the voice and the audience, the listenership. Television journalists have a personality to sell, and the personality can become incredibly valuable, if it conveys trustworthiness, for example, or even a certain kind of looks.

MG: For you, having chosen playwriting, it's a kind of super freelance. You're not beholden to anyone.

TS: No. I'm one of the people who fall into the over-rewarded category, I suppose. I don't coast on it. I work harder than I used to when I was a reporter. But it feels different. I do it for myself.

It seems to have emerged that a magazine or a publisher will do better if the product is cut into bite-size pieces, so very little gets sustained in the popular press. There are, of course, exceptions. But when People magazine first came out, I thought, 'This is not going to work: it's treating people as though they can't continue a sentence over a page. The food is being cut up on the plate for people who aren't very good at eating.' Of course I was completely wrong. I believe it was a success from the word go. It's exactly what people want. They want someone to do it all for them.

MG: You could extend that to theatre, to Broadway, where producers want to give the audience something easy to take.

TS: That's always coexisted with the other kind of stuff. I haven't seen anything here yet, but I suppose the new Sam

101

Shepard is like other Sam Shepard plays. He hasn't thought, 'We're losing the battle here, so I'm going to do it differently.' Watching *Hapgood* at Lincoln Center is kind of perfect: 350 people watching it. That would be two-thirds empty in a Broadway house. Even among those 350 people, there'd be two, three, four empty seats after intermission, so you're actually getting a glimpse of the nightmare of a Broadway audience, where you might have 50 seats empty after the intermission and a lot of people remaining doggedly to the end. And then there would be 300 people loving it in the middle of that 900. I wanted it to be done very well in a small house for a limited period, and that's exactly what has happened.

MG: How have you changed *In the Native State* into *Indian Ink*? Has it been substantially rewritten?

TS: It's been substantially added to, rather than being rewritten. I've clothed the original play.

MG: You've talked about writing a play about your growing up in India. Is this the play?

TS: No. I had talked about writing about the ethos of empire, and I suppose that's a very good example of what we were speaking about earlier: the acorn hasn't been thrown away. But it's not really just that. It's much more an intimate play than a polemical play. One kids oneself along that every little shred of reference to the larger subject resonates through the whole piece, and enlarges the play. That's just a kind of sweet thought by the playwright.

MG: In Tynan's Profile of you in the New Yorker, he spoke about your 'withdrawal from the chaos'. Did that encourage you to become more interested in politics?

TS: That was in 1977. It took a long time for him to write it and to get it into the magazine. He had worked out who I was and where I was, just before *Every Good Boy Deserves Favour*, just before *Professional Foul*, which rather spoiled the beauty of his argument. I refused to get involved in any debate about myself. I just wrote what I wanted to write next, and that's what they happened to be. I didn't think of myself as someone who had turned his back and was now halfway around again. That's the privilege of the person who's writing about you. It's quite hard to find things that you want to write a play about. So you don't question the ones that come up and hit you. You're just glad.

MG: But beginning with *Every Good Boy* and *Professional Foul*, the plays have dealt more with political issues and public concerns.

TS: Yes. But that's not true of *Arcadia*. After 1977, *The Real Thing* was next, then *Hapgood*, *Arcadia*, *Indian Ink*. Sounds to me as if I went off the whole thing after that. Except that I wrote *Squaring the Circle* about Walesa and Solidarity in Poland. It's quite hard to establish a pattern, I think. Perhaps that's the truest thing to say about me as a writer. That's a statement in itself.

I'm not sure I'm supposed to be apologetic about all this. My idea of the serious writer is roughly what you're getting at, that there's a coherent person with a programme, and the plays are all a continuation of something quite coherent. Maybe that's how one ought to be.

MG: Does it surprise you that you've dealt with so many different subjects?

TS: No. I'm a bit of a gadfly. Different things catch my interest for a while, and I have a hot flush about it, and something else catches my interest. This is why I say I feel I ought to be apologetic about it. Of course, a gadfly is not the ultimate compliment.

MG: It borders on the dilettante.

TS: Precisely. What we're leaving out: the cake is upside down. Theatre is a popular art form, it's part of the world of

103

relief and release, of entertainment. That's what it's for. The other bit of the cake which is to do with formulating and promulgating and examining and revealing – issues, life – that's a programme that can be continued through other means: journalism, television, essays. There's a case for the view that if you've chosen to work in the theatre, your fundamental objective is to be part of an art form that diverts, entertains and instructs rather than that you're engaged in teaching your fellow citizens certain lessons, which as it happens you're doing in the theatre.

MG: You said that if you wanted to change the world, the last thing you would do is write a play.

TS: What I really meant was that if there is a local concrete problem which you want to change, yes. I said that, but I'm not sure that's entirely watertight. Maybe the way to continue our conversation about newspapers would be to write a play. Funnily enough, the last time I remember the gossip columns thrown off track was by a magazine article, not by a film or a play, back around 1960. It was an article by Penelope Gilliatt, an article about the gossip columns of Fleet Street of that day. It embarrassed them, and it embarrassed the newspaper owners. The newspaper owners said, yes we have to change this, and there was a period when gossip columns became quite boring. Walter Winchell is a wonderful subject. I was kind of half-asked to write a film about him, and I really wanted to, but I thought probably it shouldn't be done by an English person. I have a little Winchell library at home, half a dozen books.

MG: Shelf life is short in all fields. But your plays keep coming back.

TS: Yes. Nothing could please me more. It's what they're for in the end. They have to have a first production, but I don't think any playwright writes for *that* production and then draws a veil and goes on to another play, which has to fill the same space. I have no idea what keeps plays alive. I suspect it's to do with the new one keeping the old ones alive. Maybe when you stop writing altogether, the whole thing will just fade.

MG: Besides *Hapgood*, is there another play you would like to do again?

TS: *On the Razzle.* It was a wonderful production. It was tremendous fun and played to packed houses for however many shows it was at the National Theatre. And then it kind of disappeared. To my puzzlement, people keep reviving *Rough Crossing*, which isn't as good a play. I think *Razzle* is an expensive play to mount. That's certainly one reason, but *Rough Crossing* is quite expensive to mount, too. *On the Razzle* was an unqualified success, but *Rough Crossing* Peter [Wood] and I got rather wrong. It's worked much better in American productions I've read about.

MG: *On the Razzle* is always shadowed by other versions of the same story, such as *The Matchmaker* and *Hello Dolly.* How did you choose to do those adaptations?

TS: I didn't. Peter Wood brought them to me and said, 'Would you do this?'

MG: The one I especially liked was *Undiscovered Country.*

TS: That was Schnitzler, not Stoppard. That was an attempt to make a faithful translation. As with Pirandello, a writer with a large body of work tends to be represented by two or three plays forever, done and redone. We wanted to show that there was more to Schnitzler than two or three well-known plays.

MG: If you had more time and the inclination, you might do another?

TS: I have no inclination, to be honest. It's nice in a way if you have nothing of your own to do. It's an enjoyable job to inherit somebody's plot and characters.

MG: Is plot still difficult for you?

TS: Can't you tell? [Laughs.] With *Arcadia* I got lucky. I didn't know it would work out like that. Like most writers – like most people – if I could live a slightly different kind of life, it would make an enormous amount of difference to how much I wrote, and the quality of what I wrote. Occasionally you get into a period where mentally you're living with this play, nothing is interrupting you, and all the the possibilities – the neurons or nerve ends – you're aware of them all and consciously or subconsciously you make the best possible use of them. If you have enough solitude and concentration, you can make the best of the opportunity. But a lot of the time I'm writing in a kind of harassed, interrupted way. I came to the conclusion the other day that the information is being fed in the wrong order in the second act of *Indian Ink*. I came back from *Hapgood* and looked at it for an hour and a half before I fell asleep. It's all done in the space of an hour here, an hour there. That's not how to do these things.

MG: You might say from the evidence that you thrive on that process.

TS: Well, no. With *Arcadia*, I had a really good period of time, where somehow I could keep it all in view and look further down the road and see where things were heading, and manipulate the material so things intersect properly. The more I got into it, the more I realised that this was going to work as a piece of storytelling. *Hapgood* was a kind of struggle from the word go and I was still dealing with it at Lincoln Center, trying to explain, simplify. We started off by referring to it as a melodrama. The way you label something is very helpful; it gets you out of the corner. Once I began to think of *Hapgood* as a melodrama, I felt much more comfortable with it, because it is melodramatic. It's not satiric about the spy business. It operates on a heightened, slightly implausible level of life. It's probably the only play I've written, as far as I can remember offhand, in which somebody shoots somebody else onstage.

MG: And somebody dies.

TS: And somebody dies.

MG: It has to work on that level for the audience to accept it.

TS: It absolutely does. The thing about melodrama is that if the audience make the right decision about it, they accept everything. If they make the wrong decision about it early on, then the drama actually becomes silly.

MG: How would you categorise *Arcadia*?

TS: Because I was happy with it anyway, I didn't need to label it. I didn't need to get myself off the hook.

MG: Some people think it's your best play.

TS: I know they do. I think that's what they're talking about: the story works best.

MG: Did you feel that you got it more together than in other plays?

TS: I did, yes. *Professional Foul* was another one; it seemed like that. The other kind of play – *Travesties* being a good example – at that time of my life, the passing show, the showing off, if you like, the pastiche and the jokes and the theatricality of it, was what the play was flourishing and boasting about. What one did was attach it to a pretty stripped down little wagon, just so that these things had some wheels to ride on. *Arcadia* and *Travesties* are like opposites of each other.

MG: And *Jumpers* is like *Travesties*?

TS: Yes, and I think *Jumpers* is a bit of a melodrama too, because it had satirical elements and melodramatic elements, but again it wasn't the nuts and bolts of the narrative that were underpinning everything, it was actually the displays of mock-erudite philosophy, philosophical jokes, all kinds of jokes.

MG: Mock-erudite?

TS: I said that because it doesn't make an original contribution. It uses what's in the marketplace of philosophy.

MG: You're not a philosopher?

TS: No, but I have a philosophical bent, I suppose. Otherwise I wouldn't bother to get interested, even on the level of what do you call it, madcap comedy. My dual personality is revealed in making value judgments on my plays. A lot of my conversation has the effect of distancing me from the nicest things said about my work. I don't want to think about my plays as being as good as some people say, or in any way important. I find that embarrassing. But anybody who writes plays wants them to be very very good, of course. And anybody who writes plays wants them to survive and be revived, to survive the writer's death, but it just seems very bad taste to share this thought with anybody else. I don't share it with anybody, not with my family, least of all them.

MG: But you know some of your plays are better than others.

TS: Of course. And in spite of defects I'm aware of and would like to correct in all of them, I also think that some of them actually are good, better than good sometimes. I'm now contradicting myself. If I have to talk about them at all, which I never volunteer to do, I'd rather use a phrase like madcap comedy, to dissemble. In a much much simpler sentence, there's a modest person hiding a proud person, I suppose. I never thought I would manage to write a play at all. It was something I wanted to do, but I was astonished when I managed to do it. Just seemed to be something that would be too difficult for me to do when I was starting out.

MG: You used to say, and I never entirely believed it, that all your characters sounded like you.

TS: I used to say it because I used to think it was true and maybe it was true in those days. I think everybody in *Night and Day* sounds like me, for example. It's less true now. It's certainly not true in *Indian Ink*. This was literally true of *Night and Day* in one isolated case: I took a speech away from one character and gave it to another, and it made no difference. I just needed somebody to say something at that point. In that sense, they were all speaking with my voice. In a limited way, you might say that they were interchangeable. So I meant it when I said it, but I wouldn't say it nowadays.

MG: It's not true of *Arcadia*, and it's not true of *Indian Ink*.

TS: No, it's not.

MG: In the New York Times crossword puzzle recently, one clue was 'the author of *The Birthday Party*,' and the answer of course was Pinter. If you appeared in the Times puzzle . . .

TS: Which play would they choose? I imagine they chose *The Birthday Party* with a certain calculation, not necessarily as the best-known play, but to make it not too easy a clue. Do you think?

MG: Perhaps. But if they wanted a really difficult clue, they would have taken an obscure play. I think they were seeking the play with which he is most identified. To answer the question, with you, they might have chosen *Rosencrantz and Guildenstern*.

TS: If they wanted to make it as easy as possible, they certainly would say that.

MG: I would think if you were being qualitative about it, you might say *Arcadia*. Through pride of authorship.

TS: Oh, I see. I would say *Arcadia*, because it's the new one. I always feel like that about the one I've just written.

MG: And soon you would say *Indian Ink*?

TS: This is where I get to my most boring. A play is not a

109

text. *Indian Ink* in a curious way doesn't yet exist as a piece of theatre. It's only something that's written down at the moment. As we know from any title from William Shakespeare, a given text can produce a satisfying, fulfilling, blah-blah evening, or one which just doesn't work at all. It doesn't matter who wrote the play. The theatre turns out to be an event which has to be carefully manipulated. It is crowded with variables which have to be put into balance. *Indian Ink* is still, as it were, a potential play.

MG: But there's a text.

TS: Yes, but before the event. The text *becomes* a record of the event, but at the moment *Indian Ink* is not a record of an event except an imaginary event. It's more like the book of instructions for the event. Once the event takes place, one can see what the text embodies, or is capable of embodying. But if we get *Indian Ink* hideously wrong, it will not be the play you will put into your crossword puzzle clue until and unless somebody gets it wonderfully right later, if that's possible.

MG: But couldn't somebody read it and not see it and get something out of it?

TS: They can and they do. But I was still going on about your crossword puzzle. They can and they do, but that is one of those arcane little private recreations that very few people have, which is to read plays. That's a tautology, I believe.

MG: About *The Real Inspector Hound*, you said it was about wish fulfilment, about 'the danger of getting what you want'.

TS: Well, I say things, don't I?

MG: Could we apply that to your life? Is there danger in you getting what you wanted, in having become an accomplished playwright?

TS: In *Hound*, it was simply about Birdboot lusting after someone onstage. I don't see it in such dramatic terms. I just feel that I was lucky. I found I could do it if I persisted. There's no danger. What's the danger? Gosh. Blessed by fortune is more like it.

MG: Years ago, at the time of *The Real Thing*, Mike Nichols said you were one of the few happy people he knew. When I mentioned that to you, you were offended by the word happy, you said that you were as unhappy as the next man.

TS: Boasting about my unhappiness!

MG: Are you a happy man?

TS: Yes. I'm just looking at the word happy for a moment. Mike was always tremendously pleased by the definition of happiness in that play. 'Happiness is equilibrium. Shift your weight.' Attaining your happiness, if you're talking about me, is learning that lesson. You try not to stand in the way of the onrushing train, to change the metaphor. But in fact I suppose what you're remembering is that happiness seems to imply a turning away from whatever might compromise your happiness. One is exposed naked in the winds of the world, and everybody around you has got problems. Some are acute, some are less serious than others. You live in the little world of your family and the larger world of your colleagues and the huge world of newspaper and television news. So happiness is not really a very adequate word. When I said I felt blessed by good fortune, that's generally the truth. Clearly your life and everyone's life is full of things that make you unhappy from time to time. You just deal with them.

MG: The onrushing train has not struck you yet.

TS: No. All my children are alive and well.

MG: Where are your children, by the way? You have four sons?

TS: Yes. One lives in Norwich. The next one is at Iver. He's making a short film of his own. The third one is in the music business, not a musician, he's on the management side. And

111

the fourth one is at university, reading French. And, touch wood, they all seem to be O.K. I have four children that are in a reasonable state. I've got a play at Lincoln Center, a play at the Haymarket. What the hell would I call my unhappiness? And yet if I say everything is terrific with me, that seems to say that Me is all that matters. It's a complicated question: are you happy? One gets visited by happiness, of course. In some other play, a character calls it 'a passing change of emphasis'. You receive these moments which might stretch for a day, where you think everything's O.K.

MG: That reminds me again of the boy in your play, *Where Are They Now*?

TS: That indeed is the play where that character says happiness is a passing shift of emphasis. I do have an idyllic vision of life. Whether one has a right to live it is another matter. It's to do with self reliance. It's cultivating your garden without being pulled, without having one's sleeve tugged by what's happening outside the wall.

MG: Could you say what Arcadia, or for that matter Eden, looks like? Is there any way to characterise an ideal state?

TS: English landscape countryside, yes. It's not my flat in Chelsea, although I enjoy being there, and I love the river outside. If one's talking about the idyllic life, it wouldn't be an urban life for me. I don't deserve it and I don't live as though I'm going to get it because I smoke a lot and I like cigarettes. But I'd like to live long enough so that anyone who is dependent on me doesn't need me anymore, and I can smoke and read my books and look at the weather.

MG: Are you still married?

TS: No, I've been divorced about four years.

MG: Being friendly with your ex-wife is a part of happiness?

TS: Absolutely. It's an essential part. If she's content, then I am.

MG: And you're still shifting your weight?

TS: I think it's a lesson I learned rather late. I'm 57. *Where Are They Now?* is a play I never think about, but it keeps coming up while we talk. There's something in there about the boy, who was unhappy at school, saying as a grown-up, 'If there was only some way to tell them it doesn't matter that much, the things that devastate you as a child, the things that spoil the whole term at school.' One would like to impart the lesson to one's children that it's really O.K., it's not as bad as you think.

MG: In *Three Tall Women*, there's a line like that: why didn't they tell us?

TS: *Zoo Story* was a play which did a lot to me. It was definitely happening in the theatre where one wanted to be. That was true also of *The Birthday Party* and *Next Time I'll Sing to You*.

MG: A number of English playwrights recently signed a letter protesting the shortage of new plays in English theatres.

TS: Eighty-seven playwrights. I refused to sign it. I read this and thought, 'This is nonsense. I hope they just go away and don't bother me.' But they wrote again, 'Please you haven't answered our letter.' So I spent an hour explaining why I didn't want to sign their letter. The more I read about it, the gladder I was I hadn't signed it. Because I just thought it missed the point and was very arrogant. I thought running a theatre and trying to make ends meet in 1994 was quite hard enough without some busybody coming in and saying what plays you had to do or not do. Whether they were right or wrong, it's not their business. How could anybody put their name to such a view of oneself?

MG: Some of your best friends did.

TS: I can't imagine what was in their minds. The main problem is that most new plays are not very good. I've judged play competitions, just the finalists, and it's rare to find one which is any good at all. My own belief is that so many people are desperately looking for good new plays that if somebody writes one, it'll get put on. The ones which don't get put on may not be worth putting on. The only danger, I think, is to writers who are so good, so far ahead, that they're not recognised. Most plays are like yesterday's mashed potatoes. The only honourable way to have one's play put on is to write one so good that people will fight to put it on.

MG: That's concluding that all good plays get put on.

TS: They do. That's my belief, unless, as I say, they're so in advance of their time that they might escape because people don't recognise what they are. Nine out of ten new plays that you see are good but not good enough, including my own. That's a side issue. The real issue is what kind of commissar mentality is it that says, 'You have to put on three new plays a year, two of them in the main house.' That completely misunderstands how culture flourishes.

MG: How do you feel about *Eleutheria*, the play that Beckett wrote before *Waiting for Godot*? He said he did not want it performed, and his executors are holding to his wishes.

TS: I'm on the side of the executors. Otherwise it renders Beckett's instructions meaningless. But why did he bother to instruct them? I don't know why Beckett would feel that he should prohibit it. Why does it matter? Obviously it would be fascinating to know what preceded *Waiting for Godot*. When I was on this panel the other day with Havel in Prague, somebody asked him how he got into theatre. He said that he read other people's classics and thought, 'Well I can't do one of these,' but when the Theatre of Absurd turned up, he thought, 'Yes, I can do one of these.'

MG: You felt the same way?

TS: No. The first play I wrote [*A Walk on the Water*, later entitled *Enter a Free Man*] was very much in the mode of *Flowering Cherry* [by Robert Bolt]. Or *Death of a Salesman*, but not in the class of either. It was a naturalistic play about people I'd never met. And then I wrote a *Waiting for Godot* type play called *The Gamblers*. God knows whether a text of that exists or not. That reminds me, I must write a letter to my executors.

February 1995

'I retain quite a nostalgia for the heat and the smells and the sounds of India'

Indian Ink, *Stoppard's stage dramatisation of his radio play, In the Native State, was in previews and was about to open in London at the Aldwych Theatre. Felicity Kendal had been in the original radio version and was returning to her role as Flora Crewe, a free-spirited, widely travelled English poet. In 1930, she visits India and has her portrait painted by an Indian artist, Nirad Das (played by Art Malik). The audience is tantalised: Flora may have posed for him in the nude. In the split time framework of the play, Flora's sister, Eleanor Swan (Margaret Tyzack), is seen in the present, reflecting on her sister's past. For the stage version, the playwright had expanded the role of an American professor who publishes a collection of the poet's letters and later becomes her biographer, offering verbal footnotes on aspects of her life and career. He also goes to India in the present to look for additional information about his subject.*

The play still focuses on the poet and painter set against the background of the approaching end of British rule in India. It is both a literary mystery and a poignant love story, raising questions about divergent cultures and codes of conduct, with Flora representing artistic and personal integrity. Vigorously, she encourages the painter to discover his own, Indian sense of identity. As artists, they search for 'rasa', an Indian word meaning juice or essence, metaphorically 'what one must feel with a work of art'.

117

Right up until the opening, Stoppard had been revising the play in consultation with his director, Peter Wood. Stoppard and I met for a quiet lunch on a busy day, in a restaurant near his Chelsea home. We began talking about the genesis of Indian Ink, which I had seen several nights earlier at a preview.

MG: I went back to the radio play looking for the differences between it and the stage play. Pike, the biographer, is now of course a more active character, and on stage there are references to many more real people, including Madame Blavatsky and Louis MacNeice. In Flora's poem about heat, there is now a direct reference to Indian ink. Did I miss any other major changes?

TS: In the middle of one of Flora's poems where there used to be a reference to a corpse in a ditch, I've now put in a woman in a blue dress sitting on a verandah writing about the weather, which is what I wanted in the first place. On Tuesday night we tried an alternative ending, and threw it out on Wednesday morning. Wednesday night you saw the first version of the ending we are now using.

MG: How different is the play from the script at the beginning of rehearsal?

TS: It's the usual illusion. We think it's significantly transformed. The audience would hardly notice the difference. You're always working on that ten per cent edge, where you're trying to make it ten per cent better. But the audience just carries away the ninety, which hasn't changed. I put in a few important things; I've taken out a few little things. We've changed the order of scenes in the second act. To us, the changes have been radical. In fact one of the scenes in the second act has gone back to where I put it originally. We're just getting in under the wire.

MG: You're locked in to the opening. The date is even printed in the published version of the play.

TS: In England, we don't postpone, unless something disastrous happens – somebody has to be ill or the scenery has to catch fire. It's a pity.

MG: When did the apricot go in to *Indian Ink?*

TS: The what? You say apricot, we say apricot. Let's call the whole thing off. The apricot was always in.

MG: But it wasn't in *In the Native State*, and it makes a crucial plot point. [Visiting the Rajah of Jummapur, Flora casually eats an apricot without peeling or washing it, which greatly impresses her host.]

TS: It was in my first or second draft of the stage play.

MG: I notice that the radio play is dedicated to Felicity Kendal, and the stage play is dedicated to the memory of Laura Kendal. Who is Laura Kendal?

TS: Her mother. She was an actress. Laura and her husband Geoffrey Kendal had a company of actors, and they toured India, as in the film *Shakespeare Wallah*. They put on Shakespeare and other plays in India and indeed in Southeast Asia. She died three years ago. I only met her when she was in her old age.

MG: Did you talk to her about India when you were writing the play?

TS: I don't talk to anybody while I'm writing. I talk a bit too much before I start. People say, what are you doing, and foolishly I tell them what I'm trying to do. It's always a mistake because I end up doing something quite different. But once I start I don't talk to anybody.

MG: When did you start *In the Native State?*

TS: It was commissioned by the BBC as a radio play. It was a completely open commission. I gave them *In the Native State* a year late. I got into my usual mess. John Tydeman, who recently retired from BBC Head of Drama, is somebody I've known since he was a young chap starting and I was a young chap starting. Periodically, they would say, 'It's about time you wrote a radio play', so I would say, 'OK.' Then I would owe them one. I like to do radio plays. I had this tiny notion that I could write a conversation between a poet and a painter. While the poet was having her portrait painted, she would be writing a poem about having her portrait painted. There would be this circular situation. That's all I had. And not necessarily in India. Unfortunately I tend to erase as I go. I don't keep a mental journal of the process.

MG: Do you remember the time when you said, why not put it in India?

TS: I don't honestly, but there probably wasn't such a point. I think simultaneously I'd been thinking about a play about the Raj, or at least India during the time of the British Empire. Things coalesced. *In the Native State* was broadcast four years ago. I was thinking about it six years ago. I delivered it at least a year after I intended to.

MG: Had you thought for many years about doing an India play?

TS: I was a child there, and it interests me. I had only been thinking about it in the general sense of using what I've got. I've got India. It feels that one should be using it sometime sooner or later.

MG: Do you have a catalogue in your head of what you've got?

TS: A little bit. Things drop off it. Hemingway was on my catalogue for years. In the end I had nothing to say about him. I never did that one.

MG: Until you learn that Hemingway met Thomas Mann in a sanatorium.

TS: Exactly. But it wouldn't be another writer. He would meet a boxer, or something, which of course he did.

MG: Here you have a painter and a poet. Although you still have your acorn about the Empire, my guess is that you think of it as an intimate play about the relationship between those two characters.

TS: Yes. But you know the footnote thing came from quite a different direction. For much longer than that I've been interested in the idea of writing a novel in which everything was actually happening in the footnotes, rather like Flann O'Brien. But pushed to the extreme, so that footnotes would be nine-tenths of the work. I don't like to think about these things, but if forced to, I suppose there is some theme of the commentator making points about the material which he is part of. The footnote idea is not that different from *The Real Inspector Hound* or *Rosencrantz and Guildenstern*. The device of having a voice outside the play, though belonging to a character in the play.

MG: The footnoting in the play seems to represent a basic mistrust of biographers. The biographer keeps getting things wrong, like Flora's reference to the Queen's Elm. He doesn't know it's just a pub on the Fulham Road.

TS: The footnote man ought to be saying that the only thing he found out was that Flora went to bed with the Rajah, which is not in fact true. I think it's very nice when the audience is ahead of the character.

MG: Does she sleep with the painter?

TS: One of the things that has been occupying us all this time is to find the point where that's a discussable possibility. Once or twice, it's gone too far for me. I had this conversation with Peter [Wood] the other day. It struck me that in the scene in which Mrs. Swan, the old lady, is saying, 'Maybe she had a romance with him, or with him, or with somebody else entirely,' it was not a scene in which the

121

audience should know more than the character. They *do* know it wasn't Durance [a young English officer], they know it wasn't the Rajah. That part of it was intentional. What was not intentional on my part was that they should *know* it was the painter she had the romance with. It's still not solved, if that's the word. But the audience seem to want it to be true.

MG: I don't think it is clear.

TS: It was clear last night, and the reason it was clear was, she woke up in bed wearing his shawl. We did that two nights. The first time the audience didn't notice. It's extraordinary what the audience refuse to notice or to listen to. She gets up in the morning and she's wrapped up in the shawl the painter had been wearing. It was some kind of browny orange dull colour, and last night we made it red, deep unmistakable red. Afterwards I said to Peter, I think that's the version for dunces. He agreed.

MG: So it's back to the browny orange shawl.

TS [laughs]: I believe there's a search on for the precise colour, which will leave half the audience completely in the dark, and the other half completely certain. I get to the point where I want to throw my hands up.

MG: The nude painting is completed before the bedroom scene.

TS: He shows it to her. And that's the moment they might or might not . . . She's terribly pleased because it's an Indian painting.

MG: A lot of the work is to know how much to tell the audience, how much to lead the audience?

TS: Yes. I'm always disappointed by the degree of explicitness which is forced out of me! Peter is a stubborn champion of an audience who are working under certain limitations. They try to take in too much at once and don't really notice things. He's constantly at me to help them. A very good example is when Flora says 'Your handkerchief smells faintly of something nice, is it cinnamon?' The last couple of nights she's actually said, 'sandalwood', which is an arc back to the first act, where he says the rasa of erotic love is stimulated by the moon, the scent of sandalwood, being in an empty house. At the end of the scene in the second act, these three conditions obtain. But I refused to let the word sandalwood appear in the scene – to everybody's fury. Two or three nights ago, I relented.

MG: So theatregoers, if they're listening . . .

TS: . . . say, 'I remember the sandalwood.' But I wanted them to remember the sandalwood by her saying 'cinnamon'. Peter thinks I'm completely crazy and perverse and out of touch with reality.

MG: You don't think some theatregoers will miss both sandalwood and cinnamon.

TS: Undoubtedly that happens. We're constantly squabbling and laughing about Brancusi. In 22 performances I think there's been only a few people who know that Brancusi is a sculptor. It makes Peter and me laugh every time Flora says, 'Ah, Brancusi,' and the Rajah, thinking it's a car, says, 'You know them all Miss Crewe.' Dead silence. But two nights ago there were two guys sitting just behind us who got everything. 'Oh yes, a Brancusi.' 'You know them all, Miss Crewe.' They went, ha-ha! Just two people in the entire theatre. Get their names! It hasn't happened again. You end up with two plays. I sort of let things happen for the Aldwych, but I'm not at all sure I'm going to give the changes to Faber and Faber for the next edition. It doesn't matter if everybody doesn't get everything. I was sitting next to three Indian people last night, who understood the Hindi in the play, and so they would have little chuckles. No one else knew what the servant and Nirad Das were actually saying because it was in Hindi.

MG: Do you understand Hindi?

TS: Not at all. I allow the actors to write those lines.

MG: And you're sure they're writing the correct lines.

TS: I haven't thought of that. Maybe they're not.

MG: Perhaps they're saying, 'Why doesn't the playwright get lost?'

TS: Or 'Why are we saying this stuff?'

MG: For you, there's a strong theme of rasa through the play.

TS: I think Peter Wood is a rasa man. I think the play works quite nicely as a series of conversations, but Peter, with his ear for music, and Carl Toms [the scenic designer] are quite a team, and Mark Henderson, who lights the show. I sat watching it one afternoon and said to Peter, 'I have this awful feeling that Mark Henderson is the cleverest person on this show, including me and you.' He never says anything, mutters into a microphone, and it all starts looking like a beautiful painting. There's a lot of rasa in those things.

I'm much more of a theatre animal than a literary animal. It's the equivalent of the potter and the clay. I just love getting my hands in it. Clearly there are many writers who can mail the play in. They write it, and that's what it is. It stays the way they write it, I am told. I think they miss all the fun. I change things to accommodate something in the scenery, or something in the lighting. Happily. I love being part of the equation. I don't want it to be what happens to my text. I like the text to be part of the clay which is being moulded.

MG: Could you say what you've learned about the play by seeing it on stage with actors?

TS: I've learned about its benevolence. One of the things that is nice about working on *Indian Ink*: there are no villains in it. It's a very cosy play in many ways. I think it's worryingly cosy sometimes. But I really enjoy its lack of radical fierceness. It has its checks and balances. There's no ranting or storming around; there are no long monologues.

MG: Is it the first cosy play about the decline of the Empire?

TS: I'm the only person in England who never saw *The Jewel in the Crown*. I keep meaning to buy the video so I can sit down when I have ten hours, and watch the whole thing.

MG: Did you read the books?

TS: No. I haven't read any of Paul Scott. I think I bought all the books, including *Staying On*, but I never read them. I keep meaning to get around to them.

MG: Because in the stage play, you made the present much more of a presence, I thought more of the relationship between it and *Staying On* as well as *The Jewel in the Crown*. You're doing a double-header in one play, where it took Paul Scott five books and his television adapters twelve hours.

TS: The play is necessarily sketchy of course. It takes a bite out of half a dozen different apples. Or apricots, as the case may be.

MG: You focus on fewer characters and on your intimate situation.

TS: Mostly, but when the curtain call comes and I see sixteen people line up to take a bow, I'm kind of amazed. This huge amount of people.

MG: It's interesting that you didn't see or read *The Jewel in the Crown*. One of those academic footnoters will say, obviously *Indian Ink* is influenced by Paul Scott.

TS: I re-read *A Passage to India* at some point. But my reading was largely factual: autobiographies, biographies, histories. I ended up with a lot of books about India but no fiction. There's the *Autobiography of an Unknown Indian* by

Chaudhuri, 900 pages, a wonderful book. Mark Tully of the BBC wrote a book called *No Full Stops in India*. I looked into two of Naipaul's books about India. Charles Allen's *Scrapbooks of the Raj* are wonderful source material: picture books of old photographs and advertisements from the time. But I had read a lot of books about India before I was ever involved in writing a play about it.

MG: I thought it was daring to mention *A Passage to India* in the course of the play.

TS: No, it was necessary. Otherwise, it's hanging over the play like an unacknowledged ghost. It turned out to be rather convenient. I set the play in 1930 without thinking about the fact that *A Passage to India* had been published in 1924. I think I felt, well I'd better get this one out into the open.

MG: How did you feel about *A Passage to India* when you read it again?

TS: I've always thought it was a wonderful book. I love Forster. He writes the sort of novel which is the only kind of novel I wish to read at all when I'm in the mood to read a novel. If I feel like reading fiction I find I really don't want to read the newest fiction. I like to go back to rather well-trod paths, with some exceptions. I want to read for the first time books of a period which I've never read. I read for solace rather than for stimulation.

MG: I wonder if people go to the theatre for solace rather than for stimulation.

TS: Perhaps. Does the Raj mean anything in America at all?

MG: It does, at least through *A Passage to India* and *Jewel in the Crown*. As you know, your actor Art Malik played one of the leads in *The Jewel in the Crown*.

TS: Did he? I didn't know that. I know he was the villain in Schwarzenegger's *True Lies*.

MG: Let's get back to rasa.

TS: I never heard of rasa until I was writing *In the Native State*.

MG: Where did you find it?

TS: In a book about Indian art. It's quite alarming how casually one trawls the ocean for things that end up important in one's work. I was looking through various books in a shop on Charing Cross Road. In the back of this book, I saw these tables of different rasa, of what the colour was and what the god was. It became very important to the play. I wasn't engaged in a systematic search, it wasn't something I would have inevitably come across. It was simply a case of being early for an appointment and going into a bookshop to kill some time. That's a bit alarming. I had already started writing the play.

MG: What if you had not found rasa in a bookshop?

TS: Well, the play does not contain all the things I didn't find.

MG: But some things you didn't find are less important than others, and this became a central image in the play.

TS: Yes.

MG: Now that you know the term, have you often found rasa in art – either in work you've seen or you've created?

TS: It's in danger of turning into another key which opens every lock. Rock 'n' roll has rasa as far as I'm concerned. It creates an emotion in the listener. It's not just for fine art. I think there is an eastern element in it which we probably don't exploit, which is to do with the state in which you put yourself into in order to receive the art. Indian music to a western ear probably goes on too long, with too little variation. I'm getting out of my depth here. The word is actually ras, juice. I took my spelling out of the book that I found. There was a lot of discussion among two or three of the Indian actors, who were puzzled and didn't think there was such a word as rasa. We went back and forth, saying ras and rasa for a week or two .

MG: Is there more rasa in the nude?

TS: Probably. I imagine so. Flora says she preferred being painted in the nude. She had more rasa. But then I just write the dialogue. I haven't talked to any people who've been painted.

MG: By having the biographer go back to India in the present – how do you feel that adds to the play?

TS: I think it justifies the play, a play which which would otherwise float between India then and an old lady in a garden in a London suburb now. Just thinking of the theatrical dynamics, it gives the play a big kick when it needs it. Fifty minutes in, suddenly there are a lot of neon signs and traffic noise, and a character who is in one part of the play turns up in another part of the play.

MG: That reminds me of *Arcadia*, where you have the converging of time and place.

TS: It's very like *Arcadia* in certain ways. But in *Arcadia* the two periods don't dovetail until the last part of the play. We're dovetailing from two minutes into the evening. The thing I like – I'm not sure we've achieved it yet – when Flora appears to tell Pike to shut up. That's quite a difficult thing to pitch right, because she's not really doing that. But I like the audience to think, oh my god, the playwright's gone mad. For a moment. In *Arcadia*, they drink from the same wine glass, things like that. They don't address each other.

MG: Emily Eden does exist?

TS: Yes. She came up in the fishing net. I had never heard of her.

128

MG: Do you have a large net?

TS: It's a question of how large the mesh is, rather than the net. I read the entire two volumes of Emily Eden and the whole thing was worthwhile for the one thing [the excerpt that ends the play and includes the line], 'I wonder why they do not cut all our heads off, and think no more about it.'

MG: One change between radio and stage is that a phrase about Indian ink now appears in Flora's poem.

TS: Indian ink is in the radio play as the title of Flora's posthumous volume. I had no thought about writing a stage play about Flora Crewe until somewhat later. People kept telling me the radio play was good and I should do something more with it. And then I thought *Indian Ink* was a good title so I put it into her poem. That's the way round. It's a curious combination of holy inspiration and the work bench.

MG: The last time we talked you said you always put a character named Chamberlain in your plays because your secretary's name had been Chamberlain. This was the first time I was aware of that while watching a play. [Joshua Chamberlain, an offstage character, has given Flora letters of introduction to people in India.]

TS: Chamberlain's got a very big role in this one. On the other hand in other plays she's not always offstage. She's offstage in *Hapgood*, just a man in a taxi. But in *Dirty Linen*, she's onstage [as a member of Parliament]. Joshua Chamberlain is the Byron [an important offstage character in *Arcadia*] of *Indian Ink*.

MG: He's not to be confused with Neville Chamberlain.

TS: He probably is every night, for all I know.

MG: Flora has poured a pint of beer over the head of a critic named J. C. Squire. Is he imaginary?

TS: No, he's a real person. He was the Literary Editor of the New Statesman and the Editor of the London Mercury. Sir John Squire, died in '58. Poet and critic, a bit of a cricket-playing, none of your arty-farty type of poetry. He stood for the Real England. He was actually an ebullient and well-loved man, I believe. Squire would have certainly thought Ezra Pound was insane. You can't really tip the audience off as to the distinction between characters who existed and characters that did not. I'm very pleased to have Emily Eden's portrait in the theatre programme. There are people who probably think Flora Crewe existed, for all I know.

MG: Do you have any memories of India, besides the one about going back to your school?

TS: I have many memories of India, all of them vivid. We lived in Nainital when we first went there. I remember being young in Lahore and in Cawnpore for a time, and Calcutta and Delhi, and finally Darjeeling.

MG: Your father stayed in Singapore and was killed.

TS: Yes.

MG: And your mother ran a shoe store.

TS: We were Bata people in Czechoslovakia. Bata shoes. We were in a group of Bata mothers and their children in India. They didn't know what to do with us. My mother got bored, and we ended up in Darjeeling. She was manager of their shoe shop. After the war, she married my stepfather, an officer in the British Army.

MG: Do you often find your past revisits you?

TS: Sometimes it seeks me out. I don't go back to my past. I've never been back to the school I left in Yorkshire when I was 17. I haven't kept it in my luggage at all.

On the afternoon before the opening of Indian Ink, we met at the Aldwych Theatre. Stoppard seemed to be in a relaxed, though anticipatory mood. He had completed his work; the rest was up to the actors – and the audience.

MG: In our last conversation, you spoke briefly about your childhood. Tell me more about your memories of India.

TS: I was there from the age of four to the age of eight, and my memories are of an Indian childhood, not a Raj childhood. We weren't really Raj people. I wasn't at the posh English schools or anything. I retain quite a nostalgia for the heat and the smells and the sounds of India. When I went back to Darjeeling four years ago, it was remarkably unchanged. The thing that struck me as different had to do with motor traffic. I had forgotten until I went back that Darjeeling had been redolent of horse manure and the sound of horses' hooves and all that. I didn't recall much traffic. Now it's got lots of four-wheel-drive Land Rovers and Range Rovers. The horses are a tourist attraction on the mall. My memories are of a rather free childhood. I wasn't very supervised.

MG: Does that mean you rambled and roved?

TS: Up to a point, yes. But that was also true of my childhood in England. Things have changed quite a lot in that respect, wherever you grow up. When I was eight or nine years old in England, I used to go off with my brother and friends and camp overnight, make rafts to float on lakes: things I would never have let my own children do. I would have been too worried for them.

MG: As an adult, you're still rambling and roving.

TS: No. I'm sedentary now. I try to travel as little as possible.

I travel when necessity makes me travel. I don't travel for its own sake.

MG: Do you have any memories of your father?

TS: I've got dim memories of him, reinforced by photographs. I have distinct, isolated memories of my childhood in Singapore. I remember being there with my mother and father.

MG: Despite the dislocation from Czechoslovakia to Singapore to India to England, was it a good childhood?

TS: Very. It was a fortunate childhood. I found English prep school life partly wonderful. It ought to have been entirely wonderful, but there were odd aspects of boarding school at that age that sometimes made me feel depressed, longing for the holidays, and a bit homesick, usually to do with the severity of one or two of the teachers. I remember thinking at the time, if Mr. Soandso would leave, life would be absolutely fine.

MG: When I talked to V.S. Naipaul about your play, he said, 'He's a refugee, isn't he?' That was a term I never heard applied to you before, but I suppose it is an applicable word. Did you ever feel like a refugee?

TS: I don't think one thinks like that at that age. One accepts one's fate. We were refugees in a way in India because we had no choice about leaving Singapore or indeed about where we were going. We got on a boat going to Australia. For some reason while we were at sea the boat decided to go to India.

MG: Ever since you came to England, you've been English.

TS: Rather before. I was educated in English. It was my first tongue, from the time I went to India.

MG: Were Felicity's parents travelling with their theatre company when you were India?

TS: Yes. Felicity actually performed on the school stage of the boarding school I was at in Darjeeling. It was after I left. I left at the beginning of '46, the year before she was born. When I went back to the school on this visit, I sat in the auditorium. I remembered seeing things on that stage, but I had no idea what I had seen.

MG: Do you have any memories of early theatrical experiences?

TS: Not in India. When I was in England I used to go to the local amateur dramatic society productions in the village hall. When I was a young journalist I used to report on amateur drama. Subsequently I would go to productions at the Bristol Old Vic and at the second professional theatre in Bristol, which was called the Little Theatre. That was really after I left school, when I was 17, 18, 19.

MG: What is your mother like?

TS: That's a very difficult question to ask a son. I've always been very close to her, and people always like her. She's very charming. She's a bit nervous in her old age. She's very anxious about all her children [in addition to his brother, Stoppard has a half-brother and half-sister]. She's a bit of a worrier, but she has a tremendous spirit, and I would say I inherited her sense of humour. She's a witty woman.

MG: In a newspaper article, John Tydeman used the word 'gestating' to describe your creative process.

TS: I think that's accurate enough for the process that gets you to the top of page one. I feed it as well. I think about it and rethink, even make some false starts.

MG: Were there many false starts on this play?

TS: It's not so much a matter of false starts. I sort of slap down anything just to remind me in a crude form of the thing I'd be interested in doing. And sometimes I write a few lines or a little encounter which fits in later on in the play. That's rare. Usually I write the plays in the order in which people see them.

MG: In this case, it would have been the scene in which she is sitting for her portrait.

TS: Exactly. I suppose the first thing I wrote was the poem which starts the play because I knew I was going to end up having to write a poem for her.

MG: Do you feel comfortable writing poetry? Do you write poetry?

TS: Occasionally, for domestic consumption.

MG: What does that mean?

TS: I don't write for publication.

MG: For birthdays and anniversaries?

TS: That sort of thing, yes. Comfortable is a word that needs examining. I'm comfortable in the sense that I'm easy in my mind, because I'm usually doing it with no volition except my own. But do I find it difficult? Yes, very. I don't consider myself in any way a poet. I make up my rules as I go along. I just try phrases, and if I hit upon a rhyme which pleases me I'll try to make the rest of it rhyme. If I hit upon a half-rhyme which pleases me, I'll do that. If it's purely a matter of cadence and word value with no detectable rhyme, I'll just carry on that way. I'm not a sensible poet in any way.

MG: Poetry is more difficult than playwriting?

TS: The poems which come off – I don't mean mine – always

seem to be little miracles. There's a collusion of sound and sense which relies on an extreme fortuitousness in the language. I think collusion of sound and sense is essential to a good poem, which is why poetry is notoriously difficult to translate. Think of any Larkin poem. I think in poetry one allows oneself a kind of literary image which in a play, in dialogue, would be too self-aware. Since we mentioned Larkin, there are wonderful things: 'a steamer stuck in the middle of the afternoon', isn't it? – somebody looking out to an ocean from a beach, or 'the trees are coming into leaf like something almost being said.' Even in Chekhov, if you had a young frustrated woman saying, 'Oh look at the trees, they're coming into bud like something almost being said,' you would say, 'Oh what an interesting way for someone to speak.' Poetry does give you that permission.

MG: Do you intentionally filter poetry, or lyricism, out of your plays?

TS: Yes. On the other hand, I've occasionally tried to let the whole thing go right through the play. I started off that way with my first radio plays, *Albert's Bridge* and *If You're Glad I'll Be Frank*. There was blank verse in long sections of them.

MG: When you write a play today, are you watchful of the language not becoming too lyrical?

TS: I think the customs officers are quite alert, so the lyricism doesn't get past them. Self-regulation. For me, I would have a deeper satisfaction and a sense of self-satisfaction if I were ever able to write a poem which was anthologised by someone whose standards were severe. I think that would be a greater achievement than any of my plays. My version of retirement is to be a poet, by which I don't mean that I want to stop work, because I love work, but my ideal form of retirement would be to spend six months on a poem, which I then wouldn't have to show anybody.

MG: You've written only one novel, *Lord Malquist and Mr. Moon*. Have you thought about writing another one?

TS: A publisher called Anthony Blond, who must have been aware of my short stories, simply commissioned the novel. At that age, at that stage of one's career, one doesn't let the opportunity go by. It's hard enough to get a publisher interested in a novel which is completed, let alone having a publisher commission a book, so naturally I wrote a novel. I haven't wanted to write a novel since, though my head is full of superior junk which I think I could turn into some kind of a chapbook, or perhaps an extended essay in the form of a chapbook with links. I feel that there is a repository in hard covers, which one day I ought to use for the things I'm not going to be able to use in my plays. Years ago Faber and Faber tried to tempt me into putting together a collection of my journalism. I'd written the odd essay for TLS years ago, and other things for newspapers and magazines. They assembled it, and I didn't think it was good enough. I don't really want to be one of those people who drags up their journalism. There are people who do that awfully well. I've never handed anything in to a newspaper or magazine without being rushed and furious. I'm usually angry with myself for agreeing to do it. I end up doing it and in it goes. You could probably find 50 pieces I've had published in different places, but God help me I don't want anybody to read them now.

MG: Playwriting is a profession that suits you?

TS: Yes it is. I think we were speaking about this the other day. Being a playwright, at least a playwright like myself, who likes to roll up his sleeves and be part of the process of getting the event organised, it's tremendous fun, and in the latter stages of it, you're living a kind of life which reminds me much more of journalism than of writing for the theatre. The page is going at midnight, or this won't fit, or we need a piece about him, can you make it four inches longer or shorter? The last part of getting a play on is completely different from the months you've spent writing it in the first place. There I don't show it to anybody, and I do it exactly the way I think it ought to be. Once it becomes shared with the actors, the director and the designer, the person doing the music and the lighting and the audience, then it turns into a different kind of creative activity, which I enjoy very much. You have to be careful with yourself not to compromise what you've already done.

MG: Earlier you said *Indian Ink* wasn't a play until it was performed.

TS: I've been saying that for years with diminishing conviction because it turns out in fact that people do like to read plays. So there is something there on paper, and it's supposed to make sense and it's supposed to make you want to turn over the next page, so in those respects it's a piece of work. But of course if there were no theatre to write for, then I wouldn't write plays.

MG: Scenes in the published text may contradict what appears on stage .

TS: Yes, they do. Actually there is a scene in the published text of *Indian Ink* which is in the wrong place. I had been persuaded against my better judgment to move it. It's a scene where Mrs. Swan shows Anish Das the painting rolled up in the suitcase. Originally it came exactly where it comes now, in the middle of the long Dak bungalow scene which ends the first act. There was a period when the scene between Flora and Nirad Das was thought to benefit from not being interrupted. So we took away the interruption and placed it elsewhere. It was an interesting experiment, but luckily we saw it was not the thing to do. However, we did it at the time when I had to correct the proofs, so the mistake is in the first edition.

MG: How do you feel about actors?

TS: I think of them as very brave. Good actors, and I've been fortunate to work at close quarters with some very good actors, I'm in awe of them. They vary of course. Some of them are highly technical, some of them work on their emotions. When I was young, I thought their job was to make the noise I had written, and then justify it in their own free time later, which was naive and silly. What one finds is they have to arrive at the right place for *them*, and sometimes it is the noise I wrote, and sometimes it isn't. Very often it is better for not being what I thought it would be.

MG: Felicity has been in a number of your plays. To what extent has she shaped the roles?

TS: With *On the Razzle*, I didn't know her, and she was playing a boy. She made it what she made it. With *The Real Thing*, I did know who she was, and it was pretty close to her modern personality, but it wasn't written for her. *Hapgood* was a difficult role which she did very well, but the one which really pleased me was *Arcadia*. She was fine when the play opened, but a month later she was absolutely individual and different from the person who had been Hannah when the play opened. She turned into somebody frumpier. I'm fairly easy-going about that side of interpretation, because I have only one concern, and that's clarity of diction. That's the only thing that matters to me, working with actors to whom clarity of diction is second nature.

MG: We've talked about your bibliophilia and about some of the books you read as background for *Indian Ink*. How large a library was it?

TS: I've probably got 50 or 60 books vaguely related. It's just a shelf and a half. I've got lots of books everywhere. I've got books on shelves, books in boxes, books in storage.

MG: Are there are any other philias in your life besides biblio-?

TS: Since childhood, I've had periods when I've done a lot of fly-fishing, trout fishing, and I'm sure I'll go back to that again. I stopped about five or six years ago after ten years of doing lots of it and ten years of doing none of it.

MG: Any phobias?

TS: No, I don't think I have . . . Television, breakfast television. There's a whole world of television that passes me by. There are people who are very very famous in England on soap operas. And people who have got huge careers which start at 7 am and finish at 10 am. They might as well not exist as far as I'm concerned. When I was younger, I used to like a lot of television. I used to watch the middle range series of cop shows, or whatever. I'm not saying I don't watch them now because they're terrible. I'm sure some of them are very good. But when it comes to a choice, I never choose to turn the television on.

Twenty-five or thirty years ago, the one-shot play on television was an important part of my life. *Armchair Theatre*, and so on. I'm very choosy now. I'm very amused by what happens to the titles of things when they cross the Atlantic. In England, the generic titles are very boring and unprepossessing. We call things 'The Tuesday Play'. Or 'The Play on Two'. Then they cross the Atlantic and they come out with these banners on them saying 'Masterpiece Theatre' or 'Great Performances'. In England, you might have a production of *Hedda Gabler*, and it's called 'The Tuesday Play'. Then you go to New York and there's somebody in an armchair by a roaring fire introducing 'Masterpiece Theatre', and it turns out to be *Miss Marple*. Everything is hyped up with the labelling over there. Here it's very British and modest.

MG: You said you wrote an India play because that was part of your stock. Do you have many things in your stock, in your storage space?

TS: Nothing left really. I mentioned Hemingway to you. I've got a Hemingway library, and I could score very high on Mastermind. I've always been interested by the character, the personality, in combination with the work. I remember twenty years ago I was delighted when I was talking to Harold Pinter and found that he felt the same way about the

Hemingway short stories in the 20's and 30's as I did. I think they're tremendously effective and they always work for me, much more than Fitzgerald, for example.

MG: Might you then write something about him?

TS: The fact that I'm interested in something doesn't necessarily mean that I ought to be writing about it. I always *think* it means that, but it doesn't necessarily mean it. I think probably I'd like to write a different play about journalism sometime. Journalism has changed quite a lot, or there are different things to be written about it. Journalism is interesting in a rather offensive way at the moment. It's the new hooliganism. Consider the Michael Foot story a few days ago [Foot was suing Rupert Murdoch for libel for an article that said he had been a spy against England]. That's a kind of hooliganism. It's exactly what Baldwin said, 'Power without responsibility.' The charge was so pathetic. It was presented in a way that discredited itself as it went along.

By the way, I was just entranced by Michael Foot's code name being Boot. Agent Boot.

MG: You might say the Boot's on the other Foot.

Afterword

On opening night of *Indian Ink* at the Aldwych Theatre the playwright was in the audience. Edging to his seat in the middle of a row, he politely excused himself for disturbing his fellow theatregoers, and then cancelled the excuse by saying, good-naturedly, 'After all, you wouldn't be here if it weren't for me.' The truth is self-evident: were it not for Stoppard, we wouldn't have been with Rosencrantz and Guildenstern at sea in Elsinore, or with James Joyce and Henry Carr in Zurich or with Hapgood probing the quadruplicity of secret agents. Or, more to the point, we wouldn't have learned as much as we have about sci, phys, lit, phil, hort, and all the other subjects he has made theatrically provocative and profitable.

During a period of several months, Stoppard repeatedly flew back and forth between London and New York, checking in at rehearsals in both cities and fine-tuning his scripts as three plays, *Hapgood*, *Indian Ink* and *Arcadia* (in its US premiere at Lincoln Center), certified his position as a leading playwright on both sides of the Atlantic. Seeing *Arcadia* in a third production, with a different cast and a different audience, one could feel the immense stimulative quality of the work.

It is Stoppard speaking about the continuum of learning, when the tutor Septimus Hodge instructs his pupil: 'We shed as we pick up, like travellers who must carry everything in their arms, and what we let fall will be picked up by those behind.' Later in *Arcadia*, Stoppard is heard through the voice of Hannah Jarvis, the inquisitive academic: 'It's wanting to know that makes us matter. Otherwise we're

141

going out the way we came in.' The playwright's self-education has led to the audience's enlightenment as well as, of course, to its entertainment.

Acknowledgments

Those who have been helpful in the preparation and the writing of this book begin, of course, with Tom Stoppard. Others include Nick Hern, who edited and published it and its predecessor, *Conversations with Pinter*; my agent Owen Laster, and my wife Ann (for her infallible editing). The first four conversations appeared in part in articles in the New York Times: 'Stoppard Refutes Himself, Endlessly', 24 April 1972; '*Jumpers* Author Is Verbal Gymnast', 11 April 1974; 'Playwright, Star Provide a Little Curtain Raiser', 31 October 1975; 'Stoppard's Intellectual Cartwheels Now With Music', 17 July 1979. Some of the material in the introduction and in the fifth section of conversations appeared in different form in the New York Times Magazine on 1 Jan. 1984 in an article entitled 'The Real Tom Stoppard.'* The final interviews took place in New York on 3 December 1994 and in London on 25 February 1995 and 27 February 1995. My thanks also to Carol Coburn, at the New York Times in New York, and to Pamela Kent at the New York Times London Bureau.

* Copyright © 1972/74/75/79/84 by The New York Times Company. Reprinted by permission.

Chronology of Plays

1964   *The Dissolution of Dominic Boot* and *M is for Moon Among Other Things*, BBC Radio.

1966   *If You're Glad I'll Be Frank*, BBC Radio. *A Separate Peace*, BBC TV.

1967   *Rosencrantz and Guildenstern Are Dead*, National Theatre at the Old Vic; and Alvin Theater on Broadway. *Teeth* and *Another Moon Called Earth*, on British television. *Albert's Bridge*, BBC Radio.

1968   *Enter a Free Man* and *The Real Inspector Hound*, in the West End.

1970   *After Magritte*, at the Green Banana Restaurant. *Where Are They Now?*, BBC Schools Radio.

1971   *Dogg's Our Pet*, the Almost Free Theatre.

1972   *Jumpers*, National Theatre at the Old Vic. *Artist Descending a Staircase*, BBC Radio. *The Real Inspector Hound* and *After Magritte*, Theater Four, Off Broadway.

1973   *The House of Bernarda Alba*, translation of Garcia Lorca, Greenwich Theatre.

1974   *Travesties*, Royal Shakespeare Company at the Aldwych Theatre. *Jumpers* at the Billy Rose Theater on Broadway.

1975   *Travesties* at the Ethel Barrymore Theater on Broadway.

1976   *Dirty Linen* at the Almost Free Theatre.

1977   *Every Good Boy Deserves Favour* at the Royal Festival Hall. *Professional Foul*, BBC TV. *Dirty Linen* and *Newfoundland*, Golden Theater on Broadway.

1978   *Night and Day*, Phoenix Theatre.

145

1979   *Dogg's Hamlet, Cahoot's Macbeth* toured Britain; 22 Steps Theater, Off Broadway. *Undiscovered Country*, adaptation of Schnitzler, National Theatre. *Night and Day*, ANTA Theater on Broadway. *Every Good Boy Deserves Favour*, Metropolitan Opera House.

1981   *On the Razzle*, adaptation of Nestroy, National Theatre 1982. *The Real Thing*, Strand Theatre. *The Dog It Was That Died*, BBC Radio.

1984   *Squaring the Circle*, Channel 4. *Rough Crossing*, adaptation of Molnár, National Theatre. *The Real Thing*, Plymouth Theater, Broadway. *Enter a Free Man*, Perry Street Theater, Off Broadway.

1986   *Dalliance*, adaptation of Schnitzler, National Theatre. *Largo Desolato*, adaptation of Havel, Bristol Old Vic.

1988   *Hapgood*, Aldwych Theatre. *Artist Descending a Staircase*, stage version, King's Head, transferred to Duke of York's Theatre.

1989   *Artist Descending a Staircase*, Helen Hayes Theater, Broadway. *The Dog It Was That Died*, television version, Granada Television.

1991   *In the Native State*, BBC Radio.

1993   *Arcadia*, National Theatre.

1994   *Hapgood*, Mitzi Newhouse Theater, Lincoln Center.

1995   *Indian Ink*, stage version of *In the Native State*, Aldwych Theatre. *Arcadia*, Vivian Beaumont Theater, Lincoln Center.